SELF-DISCIPLINE MASTERY 2-IN-1 BUNDLE

Anger Management
+
Positive Thinking Affirmations -
The #1 Complete Box Set to Improve Your Emotional Self-Control and Control Your Anger

Anger Management:
Tame The Lion Inside of You for Good

Discover How to Improve Your Emotional Self-Control, Make Your Relationships Thrive, and Completely Take Back Your Life

By Frank Steven

Table of Contents

Introduction 6
Chapter 1: Understanding the Self 8
    Discover and Understand Your Emotions of Anger 8
    Psychology of Anger 10
    Rewind, Rethink 13
    Identify the Trigger of Your Anger 15
    Admit Your Anger 18
    Face Your Anger 19
    Explore Your Fears and Insecurities 21
Chapter 2: Manage Your Source of Anger 23
Chapter 3: Take Control of Your Anger Today 35
Chapter 4: Self-Management for Better Mental Health 51
    Why Is a Good Sleep Important for Anger Management? 56
    Best Routines and Tips for Better Sleep 58
    Transform Your Anger into Constructive Action 62
    Into Practicing Fitness 65
    Into a New Hobby 66
Chapter 5: Tips to Handle a Partner with Anger Issues 69
    Maintain Your Cool 69
    Identify the Triggers 70
    Communicate in a Productive Manner 71
    Choose Your Battles 72
    Exercise Patience 73
    Empathize 73
    Be Respectful and Firm 75
    Seek Influence Rather Than Control 76
    Do Not Put up with Insulting and Disrespectful Behavior .77
    Walk Away 77

Chapter 6: Dealing with Children and Family Members with Anger Issues 79
   A Child with Anger Issues 79
      Set Lower Expectations 80
      Validate Emotions 81
      Differentiate Emotion and Behavior 82
      Exercise Patience 82
      Be Firm but Polite.. 84
      Take Extra Effort to Explain Their Emotions to Them.. 85
      Acknowledge the Triggers and Drivers to Anger 86
      Develop an Aggression Meter... 87
      Adopt Negative Punishment (Time-Out) Instead of Positive Punishment.. 88
      Teach the Child Constructive Ways to Resolve Problems 89
      Model Proper Anger Expression 89
      Avoid Subjecting the Child to Violent Influences 91
   Family Member 91
Chapter 7: Facts About Anger............................ 93
Chapter 8: Anger Management Goals..................... 98
   Anger Management Therapy... 99
   Persons Who Can Benefit..101
Conclusion... 103

Introduction

Congratulations on purchasing Anger Management: Tame The Lion Inside of You for Good, and thank you for doing so!

Every effort was made to ensure it is full of as much useful information as possible.

Please enjoy!

Anger has been the revered untouchable topic that few dares to address and even fewer admit they suffer from. Downloading this book, however, is the first step towards unmasking this monster that has been gnawing on the very fabric of society. It is the first step towards ensuring that you and your loved ones are free of its hold and control.

Majority of the problems in the world today can be traced back to an angry emotion; from the plastic bottle, an angry person throws into the river that ends up in a whale's stomach at sea or the child growing up without one parent because the incarcerated parent made a bad decision in a moment of anger. Every negative thing you see has originated from anger, and it is time it to do something about it.

To that end, the following chapters will discuss anger comprehensively to help you understand and address personal anger. You will also be equipped with knowledge of how to deal with angry people around you including your child, a spouse, or a family member. You will understand the anger from a psychological stand view, identify its triggers, understand how it presents itself, and realize the need to admit it truthfully. You will also receive guidance on the process of unearthing your fears and insecurities, and from which emotions of anger do these originate in most cases.

Having had a comprehensive understanding of anger and its sources, you also learn how to take charge of your mental health to prevent the buildup of stress and anxiety by getting adequate sleep, exercising, and eating healthy foods.

There are plenty of books on this subject on the market, so thanks again for choosing this one! Every effort was made to ensure it is full of as much useful information as possible. Please enjoy!

Chapter 1: Understanding the Self

Have you found yourself regretting what you did or said in a wave of negative emotion? Did you lash out at a child, a partner or a friend? Well, you were driven by anger. Many people have broken off meaningful relationships or landed themselves in the hands of the law over irresponsible things they said or did in the heat of the moment.

No matter how docile you are, you are bound to get angry at some point. Anger is a normal feeling that only needs to be expressed in the right measure and through proper channels. Since anger is quite powerful, managing it needs a clear understanding of it and proper anger management skills. Thankfully, these can be learned.

Discover and Understand Your Emotions of Anger

Anger is one misconstrued emotion. Perhaps because it is related to pain, people feel like it is wrong to experience it. Nobody likes to feel or to be around people going through this negative emotion. People avoid anger fearing that if they lash out or express their discomfort about something, others will lash back or draw away from them. In all honesty, no one wants to be around an angry person, their negative energy drains the very life out of you. However, our discomfort with anger is because we are grossly mistaken.

The wrong ideas society has about anger have caused us to perceive anger as this alien uncontrollable force that violently takes over a person and one that calls for an equally violent method to let out. Words like 'boiling up,' 'fuming', 'bursting', 'welling up' and 'blowing off some steam are used to describe the pressure and the heat that comes with anger. It is also said that it is healthier to release this violent energy rather than keeping it bottled up. However, the idea that purging is the cure for anger is highly defective.

In truth, releasing anger as we call it only intensifies, justifies, reinforces, and amplifies it. Angry people expressing themselves violently in a bid to release the emotion are likely to say hurtful words, cause destruction of property, and embarrass themselves and others, which will also aggravate those around them. When the atmosphere is ridden with negative emotions, people are barely able to come off their high emotions without help. However, once you gain a proper understanding of what it is, why it comes up and how to deal with the emotions, anger is likely one of the best emotions in a person. You are made in such a way that all of your emotions portray passion, skills and special gifts, and it is only right if you include anger among them.

To begin with, understand anger as an inherent emotion whose function is to protect and preserve you from emotional, physical, and mental abuse. Anger is also the emotion that establishes your presence, position, and dominance to the universe. It helps to establish boundaries that set you apart as an individual, as a member of a family, and as part of different social groups.

When anger is roused, it forces you to face challenges and opposition from your personal standpoint. You are able to state your position and erect proper boundaries, thereby improving your self-image and self-esteem. It acts as a trigger that restores your sense of self and helps you define yourself outside the confines of control and influence. Beyond your own boundaries, you also become angry when other people are degraded, mistreated, insulted, or any such kind of offense. It is anger that drives you to take a stand, defend them and help them reset their personal boundaries. Consider your anger sacred as it is the reset button that proves your true identity to yourself and to others.

Subtle anger also helps to define and establish interpersonal boundaries. When you know what tips off a person, you are less likely to do it to them. This maintains mutual respect and opens up communication lines as people express to each other what they like and do not like. Unfortunately, most of us are not trained to recognize subtle emotions and will wait until the anger flares up to do something about it, which makes us associate anger with pain and negative uncontrollable behavior.

The next time that you or a person around you is angry, take a moment to understand the motivation or the factors that could be driving the anger. It could be that you are trying to define your boundaries, stamp your authority, or simply prove to the people that you exist.

Psychology of Anger

As we have established, anger is a response to the pain felt when a person goes through unpleasant experiences, which means that it does not come about in isolation. However, pain is still not enough to arouse angry emotions; thoughts that ignite anger must also be present. These could be a person's assumptions, assessments, appraisals, and reading of the situations that make them believe that their counterpart intends to cause harm to them. In that case, the negative emotions are subjected to the target believed to cause them, who can sometimes be the angry person himself.

People also use anger as a substitute to avoid feeling the pain. They do this because feeling angry often feels better than withstanding pain. They do this both consciously and subconsciously. Exchanging pain for anger is thought to be advantageous because it provides a distraction. While a person bearing pain focuses on the pain he is feeling, an angry person thinks about taking retaliatory steps against those causing the pain, sparing himself from feeling the pain.

However temporal it might be, anger also saves people from having to deal with the painful reality. It is the perfect smokescreen to mask your feelings about what is happening. A situation could be frightening and causing a person to feel defenseless but getting angry is the perfect way to get the situation resolved without having to show any vulnerability. For example, in the event of death or the diagnosis of a terminal illness, being angry and blaming yourself or the circumstances adequately masks the pain of the loss of life or of health.

Becoming angry brings a sense of moral supremacy and power. It is impossible to feel morally superior when in pain but when you get angry, you are able to justify your emotions. You become angry for a cause and take a stance against those that have done you wrong. You begin to justify punishment and other negative results believing that the perpetrators deserved it. People like to be found on the right side of reason, and will likely find a moral reason to justify their anger.

Anger can be a self-sooth strategy. When angry, the brain releases norepinephrine, an analgesic (an analgesic causes pain relief or acts as an anesthetic) triggered by psychological or physical pain. When this chemical is released expressly into the body, it numbs the pain. This makes anger both a detrimental reaction and an effective coping method for emotionally vulnerable people because it helps them survive the pain. Psychologists say that this strategy sufficiently masks even the most distressful emotions such as those that are hurt to the 'core.' They include rejection, deceit, guilt, feeling ignored, accusation, powerlessness, unfitness, and feeling unloved or devalued. However, if anger is able to fend off these agonizing feelings, a person may become dependent to the point of addiction.

Psychologists also consider anger to be the shaky rail that people use to walk towards empowerment. If a person is using anger as a self-medication to overcome psychological pain, they will undoubtedly use it to overcome feeling powerless. Besides the analgesic norepinephrine that numbs pain, the brain also excretes epinephrine, a chemical that causes an energy burst through the body causing the popular adrenaline rush. This rush is what makes sudden anger attacks cause a feel-good and all-powerful feeling. Suddenly, the defenseless and destitute feelings are replaced by an intense sense of pleasure and control. This has led psychologists to conclude that if anger is able to address some of the most deep-seated issues people have every time, many people are likely to become addicted to it and in the end, it is likely to control us all.

Unbeknownst to many, anger is also a tool used in intimate relationships as a sure way to attach. Without even knowing it, people use it to maintain some distance between them and their partners. This behavior in most cases draws back to childhood where indifferent, untrustworthy, and erratic care fostered a shy, defensive attitude for the child in his adulthood. As adults, they may still yearn for secure attachments that they missed in childhood, but they are wary of expressing this desire openly fearing dismissal and rejection. They also fear that letting down their guard will make them vulnerable to jabs and attacks from their partners based on their unstable past. This is the reason why many of them to respond with anger when a partner forces them to recount their old wounds. Therefore, anger becomes a survival technique and a protective shield that keeps others from prying or forcing them to disclose any needs or feelings.

Rewind, Rethink

We have established that anger does not work alone, it originates from previous pain, and a person's assessment of the current situation. This means that anger is driven by a precise thought process. For most people, distorted thinking is a major factor in their retaining of anger. This is what causes people to differ in opinion because if one person thinks one way, another will think differently, and one event can be interpreted differently. However, if one thought process leads to this outcome, we can comfortably assume that another thought process could lead to a different outcome. Therefore, if thinking one way triggers your anger, it is likely that thinking differently may lead you to a different reaction.

It is possible for you to change your reaction to infuriating situations by changing how you think about them. Realize that you are in charge of your emotions and that no one can make you feel any of them, not even anger. You only become angry with what you think and what you say to yourself. For example, the statements "He cannot treat me this way! I will show him who I am!" do not elicit any positive energy, you are only likely to become angrier. Therefore, you can change your reaction to stressful situations by changing how you think about them without attacking other people verbally and physically, and without releasing a string of hormones that could damage your cardiac system in the long run. With a renewed mindset, instead of getting confrontational, you will prudently find a solution to the issue.

Having the same negative reaction to unpleasant results could lead you to develop chronic anger that could harm your health. This is because anger takes up so much energy and this constant withdrawal is stressful to the body. People who get angry at minor frustrations and irritations end up altering their psychological and physical wellness. It also causes recurrent arguments and physical aggression that will undoubtedly ruin social relationships and deter improvement. It is unlikely that you will climb up your career ladder by giving your boss a tongue-lashing.

Just to emphasize, it is imperative for you to know that the things we go through in life depend on our interpretation of what bombards us. If you interpret a careless or unintentional remark as a deliberate attack on your person, you will end up using the nasty remarks as a catalyst to fuel your anger. While the person could have also truly meant to put you down, it is your thoughts that will drive you to anger. To prevent this, put up a filter that separates what comes in and what happens in your mind. Do not let the ungraciousness and crudeness of others spoil your day. Be cool, think sober thoughts, you will be fine.

Identify the Trigger of Your Anger

Rather than dealing with anger and its effects, it is easier to work towards preventing the flare-up from happening in the first place. They say prevention is better than cure. To get ahead of the anger, you must understand and correctly identify its triggers. Once you do so, you will be able to respond to them better because you will be hands on.

Each person is wired differently, which means that what tips off one person may not do the same to another. Triggers are primarily dependent on the life experiences a person has had. For example, a person who was abused physically or emotionally as a child will quickly develop anger when subjected to words or actions that threaten their physical or emotional well-being.
The general understanding, however, is that people anger more easily when they are annoyed, hungry, lonely, or tired. If these feelings are present, it does not take much to tip them off.

Below are some anger triggers.

- *Disappointment and dishonesty*: Like me, most people are tipped off by dishonesty. When a person tells a lie, you will wind up upset, annoyed, and angry when the truth comes up. Others make promises and do not live up to it. You will feel also betrayed and angry when a partner cheats, a colleague uses dishonest means to bypass you for a promotion, your child lies, a boss fails to promote you as promised or some conniving person brings a false accusation against you.

- *Discrimination and prejudice*: People are treated unfairly because of their class, nationality, sex, race or ethnic group, disability, sexual orientation, appearance, and religious beliefs, among others. Only a few people like Nelson Mandela and Gandhi have been able to channel the pain and anger from discrimination and prejudice to good and transformative causes. Prejudice and discrimination, whether blatant or subtle, brings a sense of unworthiness, defenselessness, and makes a person feel small. Most people respond to it with anger, despair, irritation, and rage. Amazingly, both the victim and the perpetrator suffer the same emotions. We have seen this in the viral videos where some people call the police on others based on biased reasons.

- *Unfair treatment*: Unfair treatment will undoubtedly cause irritation, annoyance, and anger toward anyone. Unfortunately, events like this occur quite often. For example, a teacher could give you a clearly unfair grade, a boss could assess your work inaccurately, a police officer gives an undeserving ticket or someone cuts the line at the movie theatre. While you are bound to feel bad, how you express these feelings determines whether they escalate or are brushed off as nothing.

- *Attacks*: The world is a violent place and more often than not, you or a person affiliated to you will be the subject of an attack. Attacks are in the form of intimidation, child abuse, war trauma, domestic violence, verbal attacks, sexual abuse, and accidents. While some people develop anxiety and depression, others become angry. For example, the recipients of chronic abuse end up becoming abusers too, in some events. Just like in the case of discrimination and prejudice, the perpetrators of attack often suffer anger just as their victims do.

- *Self-esteem threats*: Everyone wants to feel good about who they are. Even those who suffer chronic self-esteem issues like to feel good about themselves. However, a person will threaten your self-esteem when they insult or disrespect you, reject you, criticize you, fail to choose you or embarrass you in front of others. On receiving these threats, some people increasingly loathe themselves, become sad, and others become angry.

- *Time* pressure: Our world is presently a beehive of activities. People have the pressure to increase their output and to multitask, but inevitably, there will be things that get in the way. For example, running into traffic when hurrying to get to work, having your call put on hold for a long time, a partner or a friend constantly sending you text messages while you are busy at work or having to go through thorough security checks at the airport while getting late for your flight could make you frustrated.

Below is a summary of anger triggers discussed above and others that are not discussed. This list provides a broader view of prevalent anger triggers. (Kindly copy the list and check those that apply to you. Managing anger will start by identifying the triggers. Add any other triggers as you recognize them).
- Lies
- Misunderstandings in relationships
- Injustice
- Offensive words
- Disappointment
- Threats

- Infringing on personal space
- Disrespect
- Insults
- Distorting information
- Inappropriate Labels

These triggers will be a starting point for you to understand the things that cause a high alert in your brain, and once you have identified and understood them, you will be prepared to handle the situation better than you did before.

Admit Your Anger

When you admit something, you declare that you have full knowledge of it and are in control. Naming and admitting, also called recognition, go hand in hand. It is impossible to recognize something without giving it a name, and you only name things that are in your knowledge. For example, when you hear a very loud deafening sound in the sky, you will be very frightened and will report that you have heard a very scary loud noise. However, once you have a name for it, you are in full control of your fears. You can differentiate between the sound an airplane makes when flying overhead and the sound of a thunderstorm. Both are loud and frightening, but you no longer fear because you understand each.

This concept applies to every other thing in life. Once you name and recognize/admit it, you will have more control over it and over how you feel about it. When you admit your anger, you realize that you are angry, understand what has triggered the anger, and are able to control it.

Knowledge and admitting anger also influences how you communicate your anger. There is a splitting difference between communicating knowledge that you are angry and communicating the feeling itself. If you want to communicate your anger, you will speak like this, "You underage pothead, pack your clothes and leave my house!"

When you speak like this, you have communicated your anger, which means that you have given in to an unknown feeling, that you do not understand, and let it control you. However, if you intend to communicate the 'knowledge of anger', you will speak like this, "I feel very angry and cannot speak to you right now. Perhaps you could leave my house and we can talk about it when I feel calmer."

The first and the second statement are very different. The first only shows that you are experiencing the feeling, but the second shows that you are in full knowledge of what is going on and can still communicate what you feel. In the first example, you would expect that a person saying these things will throw things around or is preparing himself/herself to beat the child. However, in the second example, the person is probably sitting in a chair thinking about what has happened, processing his feelings, and contemplating the action to take. The second person has control over his or her feelings than the first.

When you admit your anger, you take control of your emotions, make others see that you are firm in your decisions, and avoid making unnecessary rash judgments that could cost you in the future.

Face Your Anger

I once heard the story of a woman who forgave the man who killed her only son. She visited the man in jail, hugged him, and allowed him to rent the space next to her house after he had served time. This story sounds bizarre to many people who would beg the judge to issue the man a life sentence without parole, or better yet, a death sentence. However, this is not how facing your anger works. It is likely that the woman admitted, accepted, and faced her anger before concluding that no amount of retaliation against the killer could bring her son back. This is beyond taking the high road, but yeah, it only happens when you come face-to-face with your anger and overcome it.

Anger makes you feel like you have the right to revenge without requiring you to restore or repair what has been damaged. It introduces the concept of payback, which is an urge that people get, nudging them to restore 'cosmic balance'. It is an attempt to overcome the helplessness they feel by displaying their ability to control the situation. However, a retaliatory response only provides a temporary false sense of relief and prevents you from dealing with the pain within.

A person with an overwhelming sense of entitlement is open to anger displays. To him, expressing rage is a means to acquire control and to affirm his status as a boss, a parent, a husband, or otherwise. It is an attempt to dominate. However, the higher the expectations, the more upset the person will get when demands are not met. Nevertheless, history will tell you that those who are deeply wronged often do not carry any resentment. They have learned to rewrite those feelings to avoid being swayed away from the important task or mission at hand. Nelson Mandela, while writing in prison, said that enmity and hatred is a trap laid and that when you fall into it, it becomes difficult to differentiate you and the adversary.

In not so many words, facing your anger is simply rising above it. This does not make what has been done insignificant; it only makes you realize that there are more important things at stake. It keeps you in control of your emotions so that you do not allow a moment's fury to ruin the natural course of things. When you let go of your anger, you let go of the need to take control, which brings more peace than making sure that people shape up to meet your demands. It does not mean that people will not face the repercussions of what they have done. If people are being sloppy in their job, their performance will show soon enough. However, for your peace of mind, let go, and rise above the negative emotions. You are worth the peace that comes after.

Explore Your Fears and Insecurities

Fears and insecurities bar you from understanding yourself or the situation fully. It brings paranoia and anxieties, leading you to make harsh judgments, have lofty expectations, and avoid taking positive action. You fear criticism, judgment, rejection, unworthiness, and avoid being yourself around others. You begin to assume that everything is a direct attack. You are also likely to develop unhealthy attachments to people and use them as tools to build your self-worth and self-esteem, praying that they will only see the best in you. However, everyone is bound to make a mistake and in reality, even the people you have esteemed so much will let you down.

Most people that lack confidence naturally compensate with arrogance, cockiness, selfishness, and competition, particularly in social settings. Others become combatant, defensive, and willing to blame others for their problems. They blame others for their mistakes, are roused to jealousy, and can be very aggressive. These behaviors are not the real person; it is only an attempt to hide insecurities. This is an awful way to live because it puts you to the task of constantly hiding and masking your true self.

Unfortunately, there is not a nicer way to resolve fears and insecurities than to deal with it. People say that it is all in the mind and it is true. The problem is that you think about it too much. Have you seen someone in with a disability or a deformity that they embrace? You tend to fall in love with the person and admire their life, but guess what! Most often than not, the deformity or disability was once an insecurity that the person learned to embrace and suddenly, the world loved it too. You might also have been bullied for something, but embracing it begins to radiate beauty.

But of course, if it is something you can change, take the first step today. You will be happier with yourself, your progress and will be less prone to anger. See the peace and joy that will follow.

Chapter 2: Manage Your Source of Anger

Feelings do not just come up, they must originate from an event, a person, or an object. You could trip on your way to work and the embarrassment from that could leave you tipped off all day. A surprise gift in the morning can make you jolly all day so that you overwork, however, you still end up happy at the end of the day. Since the feelings you get do have an origin, working through anger will be more effective when you can trace it.

To determine the origin of your negative emotions, do the following:

- Discover Your Past Unmet Demands

    Anger is the iceberg that signals something bigger lies underneath. Most times, when you are feeling overwhelmed, frustrated, angry and sad, it is because a need you had was not been met. The unmet need needs voicing or acknowledging, and will constantly resurface nudging you to make peace with your past. The constant tagging slowly turns into anger that is roused at the slightest provocation. It also brings up fear and anxiety that keeps you on edge, worrying about whether or not others will find out about your insecurity.

    Some people's unmet needs date back to experiences they had in their childhood. The pain from an experience keeps gnawing at them as they regret why they did not run away, speak up or take other proactive steps to stop the abuse or unfair treatment they went through. Others remain fixated on the feeling of helplessness they had while going through the terrible situations they did. This numbing pain can prevent the person from becoming an effective guardian or parent. It can also cause them to withdraw from their family forever.

The most agonizing of these pains is the pain of disappointment when let down by people who are close and were supposed to be a source of support. Many times, people that you count on to help you at a time when you are most vulnerable do not rise up to the occasion. You may have heard of stories where children were being abused and when they reported it to their parents, the parents dismiss it or simply do nothing to stop the abuse. Others are forced to raise themselves and their siblings while their parents are out high on drugs and alcohol. Children raised by uncaring parents and in volatile environments like these do not get to experience parental care and love, and the void that forms from this disappointment causes pain that is particularly difficult to overcome.

Along the way, we also fail to meet our needs because we hesitate to ask. Some fear to ask because they think that when they receive, they will not have deserved it; they will only have succeeded in putting pressure on the other party. This mostly happens in the workplace where you are afraid to ask for a raise or promotion in fear that your boss will grant it because of the pressure you exert and not because you rightfully deserve it. Others fail to ask because they feel that they are being needy, intrusive, and rude. Introverts particularly worry about how they will make the other party feel if they place their request.
It is also possible to have a list of unmet needs if you do

not think of yourself as needing anything. People like these attempt to hide their needs by acting fine while they could be drowning inside.

The fear of rejection and other negative reactions also drives people to suppress their unmet needs. They are frightened of hearing 'no' because it will have an effect on their person. When you feel insignificant, not good enough, or when you lack a sense of self-worth, you tend to take anything you hear personally. You develop a veil that validates your assumptions and thinking, which is sometimes not objective. The next time you feel frustrated and irritated, retreat and ask yourself one question, "What do I need right now?"

The answer to this question is not often what you are targeting your feelings towards. You could be angry that your husband forgot to buy certain items on your shopping list but really, it is only that you have attached meaning to him buying every item on the shopping list. It could be that him purchasing everything you need shows you that he cares and when he forgets, you assume that his attention is diverted to something else. Although you will still need the groceries, analyzing his forgetfulness through the lens of unmet needs will help you take note of the unmet needs, communicate about it, and work towards a solution.

- Make Peace with the past Unmet Demands

The demands of our pasts are not similar to the demands of the present or the future. While you can act on the present and the future, it is almost impossible to meet a past need today. When it comes to needs like these, instead of agonizing over the indelible pain it has caused, people are better off making peace with the past unmet needs and moving forward. People say that the past is only good for two things: to enjoy the benefits and to learn from it. If a memory does not bring any good feeling, it is best to make peace with it.

The mind is naturally conditioned to remember the past, which makes making peace with painful memories quite difficult. We stay attached to profound experiences and the accompanying emotions both consciously and unconsciously. This makes us prone to reliving them time and again, which festers wounds that add no value to the present life. However, when you consciously and decisively work towards making peace with the past, you experience freedom allows you to forgive others or yourself, move forward, and live up to your potential.

This process can be done in the following steps:

- *Look back on all those past events, however painful.* Letting go does not just involve packing the bags and putting the past behind you. The harder you try to shove your past, the harder it clings to you. Instead, relive the moments, grieve the pain from the unmet needs, the fear and the anxiety you suffered. Although this will be difficult, you will note considerable change and improvement. It may help to write down all those experiences you have kept away from or repressed. Finally, you have exposed the truth!

- *Take in the past*: When you take in the past, you

recognize the event and accept it. You do not say, "I wish my mother took time to raise me instead of going out all the time." Instead, you say, "I accept that my mother did not take time to raise me."

I lost my father to cancer at a young age. It took me many years to accept his death. When I finally did, I accepted that I would have to grow up with one parent, and I was okay with it. I must warn you that comparing yourself to others will slow the process of accepting your unmet needs. Had I compared myself to my friends, who were raised in two-parent homes, I would probably still be angry and grieving many years later. Accepting your past means moving on while the gaps are still in it.

- *Look for the sparks*: Just as each cloud has a silver lining, there is good in every experience, however dark. It is difficult to see this at first, but when you become friends with your past, the cards will begin to fall in the right places and you will see the hidden treasure. In my case, I got to have a new relationship with my mom, and this would not have happened otherwise. I became stronger. I was able to comfort others who lost their parents and I now know the importance of a father. I would not dare deny my kids one. What I am saying is that had it not been for your pain, you would not be the awesome person you have become.

- *Stop blaming others*: Trying to change what has already happened is impossible. For lack of a better term, you would be crying over spilled milk. What holds back many people are the limiting beliefs they have about their past, talking about what others should or should not have done. For example, saying "My boss should not have fired me while I was pregnant" or "My mother should have kept me instead of giving me up for adoption" is not going to make you feel better. The event already happened, and as you know, history does not change.

Instead, try putting yourself in their shoes perhaps, and you will find a different explanation for what happened. For example, you could say, "My mother was financially, psychologically, and emotionally ill-equipped to take care of a baby on her own and bringing me up in this kind of environment would have been unhealthy and unfair to me." When you change how you think about it, you will be able to move on.

- *Do not seek confessions from the guilty party*: We believe that hearing a confession and acknowledgment of guilt from the offender gives closure but sometimes, this is false. Not every person will apologize; some are glad that you are suffering. In fact, no one will intentionally hurt you then do you good. This admission and recognition you seek is only an illusion because until you have dealt with your emotions yourself, you are not off the hook.

- *Forgive forget*: Forgiving is critical in making peace. It rids you off the negativity and judgment. You forgive for your benefit and not the offenders'.

- *Take caution*: Be alert and look out for negative

feelings and thoughts that may arise. If they come, let them but do not suppress or give them room. Let them pass. Each thought will tell you how you are progressing. Soon, peaceful thoughts replace painful ones.

- *Consciously let go of your past*: The last step involves your will. You consciously let go and resolve to not let your past dictate your future. Let go for real, knowing that you deserve the best. If you feel that you need therapy at this point, go for it!

- The Psychology of Forgiving Your Past

For a long time, scientists have puzzled at the concept of forgiving and forgetting, and its influence on psychology. They realized that once a victim forgives her transgressor, she is better placed to intentionally forget words and emotions linked to the offense. Those that are unable to forgive have trouble forgetting unwanted memories. Surprisingly, they link forgetting to the very act of forgiving, not just the potential to accept other people's mistakes.

Psychology studies have also found that people with higher forgiveness levels enjoy better health and report lesser cases of anxiety, depression, and anger. Even in intimate relationships with a history of betrayal, greater forgiveness levels were found to lead to more gratifying relationships. Physiologically, a more forgiving person's white blood cell count is significantly lower than that of a grudging person. The body produces white blood cells to fend off infections and diseases. These results show that it benefits both the mind and the body to forgive others.

Forgiving shows that you are putting your future in mind. In a study to determine the link between forgiveness and psychological health, scientists found that people who had accumulated much stress over their lifetime presented worse mental health issues. Among those with high scores on forgiveness measures, stress was not a significant factor affecting their mental health. This study proved that forgiveness is surprisingly more powerful than we would presume. It knocks over the link between psychological distress and mental health.

Similar studies conducted to confirm these findings often have the same result. They find that as forgiveness rises among different people, the lesser the stress levels. In turn, lower stress level lead to a good state of mental health.

The results from these studies are not only good for people who find it easy to forgive, but there is also good news for those who hold grudges. They show that forgiving can be learned, but will need a bit of practice. You will not have to achieve the highest level of forgiveness in the first attempt, but with time, you will realize that the negative emotions no longer exist. It will shed off some of your stress, and ultimately make you feel better.

Start by making effort to develop empathy. Expressive writing and journaling aimed at helping you become more empathetic will be a good place to start. In your writing, be in the shoes of those that offended you and seek to write in an empathetic tone. If you are religious, prayer helps greatly. People who pray for others are less likely to hold grudges and scheme retaliation against them. Only give the process time, do not just give up after the first attempt. Keep trying; persistence breaks all resistance.

- Detect as the Source of Anger Arises

You can detect anger as it comes up because it does not just flare up without warning signs. Anger being a typical physical response, your body prepares for it. These preparations are the tell signs that you are about to explode. Taking precautionary moves and understanding your personal anger traits helps you to get ready and take action before it spirals out of control.

The signs of anger include a sudden headache, pounding heart, faster breathing, clenched jaws and fists, a sudden flash, pacing about, tension in the shoulders and having trouble seeing.

We often think that what others do to us is what leads us to anger. However, anger is more about your interpretation of an event than it is about how you have been treated. Anger, in this case, is fuelled by placing blame, making assumptions, overly critical, obsessing on what others should have done right, and overgeneralizing. Once you are aware that you are doing any of these, quickly distract that thought pattern and focus on another important issue.

Some places, people, and situations could also provoke you to anger. However, pressure and stress are no excuse for anger. You must be in control of your surroundings and avoid unnecessary provocations. In your daily routine, identify people, places, times, and situations that make you upset and unhappy, then come up with ways to avoid them.

Below are a number of anger triggers based on the environment:

- *At the workplace*

    - Having a lower salary than a colleague as qualified as you.
    - The sight of a bootlicker who gets ahead by crude methods rather than performance.
    - The very sight of your employer.
    - Knowing more than the supervisor.
    - An unkept promise particularly related to salary increment and promotion.
    - Being asked to do something you believe to be wrong or unethical.
    - Micromanagement by your supervisor.
    - Very high expectations that are impossible to live up to.
    - Lack of proper compensation for the work you do.
    - Criticism from the boss or the client for no good reason.
    - A partner being late for an important meeting.
    - Verbal attacks and intimidation.
    - Sexual harassment.
    - Sexism
    - Racial profiling and discrimination.
    - Disrespect
    - Rejection

- Rude customers.

- *At home*

  - Disrespect from a partner or a child, and vice versa.
  - Lack of appreciation from those you care for.
  - Lack of provisions like groceries and money.
  - Domestic violence.
  - Sexual harassment and abuse.
  - A partner or a child being constantly late.
  - Attitude problems.
  - Wrong assumptions and beliefs.
  - Self-judgment
  - Rejection
  - Sexism
  - Unfair division of labor.
  - Mistrust and unfaithfulness.
  - Religious misunderstanding.
  - Misplaced anger.
  - A selfish and inconsiderate person.
  - Belittlement
  - A feeling of low energy.

- *At school (for a child with anger issues)*

  - Unfair treatment by both teachers and students.
  - Racial profiling.
  - Low grades.
  - Homework overload.
  - Disorders like ADHD and IED (Intermittent Explosive Disorder).
  - Neglect and trauma.
  - Sensory processing problems (trouble processing

information).
- Autism
- Undiagnosed and untreated learning issues.
- Comparison with other students.
- Disrespectful acts and remarks.

Chapter 3: Take Control of Your Anger Today

You have both the capability and responsibility for controlling your anger. Anger is a natural emotion, but lack of control could make life quite difficult. Each day, there are sources of anger all around you; there will be traffic snarl-ups, a carefree driver, a careless comment, or the very sight of your boss that makes bouts of anger throb at your temples. While you may have a justifiable reason for your anger, you can choose not to have a negative response by opting to do something else; take control of it.

To do this, practice the following:

- Practice to Be in the Moment, Increase Awareness of Your Emotions

    Like me, you have probably found yourself immediately regretting something you said carried away by emotions. I am known to utter some of the most snarky comments in family gatherings driven by unresolved anger over what someone did or said in the past. The shame and guilt that follows for the rest of the event; you would not envy. Everyone looks at me knowingly, as if to say that I am the wet blanket that dampens their mood. Others begin to avoid me, possibly so that I do not air their dirty laundry in public. The truth is that we all fly off the handle sometimes, and could use help managing our emotions by increasingly becoming aware of them.

    With good reason, contemporary psychology is emphasizing the importance of emotional intelligence.

This concept is associated with an improved work performance, more satisfaction in relationships, and an enhanced ability to handle stress. By definition, emotional intelligence is the ability to control and to be aware of your emotions and developing empathy for others. Once you are aware of your emotions and those of others, you are able to run relationships more effectively and be in control when conflicts come up.

Emotional awareness is founded on self-awareness. You get a grip of your emotions when you gain a deep understanding of who you are and how you come off to others. You are able to understand your feelings any time and can identify their source. You are also able to identify physical manifestations of anger such as a sudden headache, an increased heartbeat, or sweaty palms and are able to act on your emotions immediately.

Increasing your level of self-awareness is simple. Begin by taking some time off to study you. Yes, you will study you. Take some time to carefully monitor your emotions. Give an honest answer to questions like "How do I feel now? What causes me to feel this way? How is my body manifesting this feeling?" Once you identified the emotion that you are feeling, label it. Is it anger, anxiety, or fear? Write this feeling down along with what you think could have triggered it. Once this information is on paper, it is now easier to identify what you are dealing with, and you can begin to strategize on what to do to overcome the negative emotion.

Once you are aware of what triggers you and have a response strategy in place, it is time to keep alert in case some emotion pops up. This is what we call mindfulness, or 'being in the moment'. It is simply being very alert to listen to what your feelings and emotions could be whispering to you at any moment. You consciously and actively pay attention to the happenings of the present. When you live in the moment, you realize that you are only an observer of your thoughts and that they do not make you. You only let them slide without suppressing any. It allows your inner being to awaken and experience life, instead of simply going by it.

Developing this awareness holds a number of benefits for you. It will reduce stress, lower pain levels, improve immunity, lower blood pressure, and help you cope with terminal illnesses and the pain from past unmet needs. Once you able to spend time enjoying the moment, you also reduce your susceptibility to heart illnesses. Your body and your mind will begin to feel like happy places for your soul to reside.

When people are mindful, their lives improve significantly. They become more happy, empathetic, and secure. Their self-esteem soars and is more accommodating of their shortcomings. Negative coping behavior, reactivity, and impulsivities like binge eating, attention problems, and depression begin to come down. There is also less fighting in relationships because the people become less defensive and more accepting. It becomes easy to let go when verbally attacked because they realize that not all battles are worth fighting. For these reasons, mindful people have better relationships with others.

As you work and focus on being mindful, do not do it just for the benefits. When you do something expecting results, your focus your mind on the future, and this beats the entire concept of living in the moment. Instead, do it step-by-step knowing that benefits will set in whenever. For now, focus on knowing you.

- Stop and Think Before You Speak/Act

When you are angry, you talk intending to communicate something, but most importantly, to express how something has made you feel. However, when emotions are running high, it is easy to let out a careless statement without thinking about it. You only realize that you said something hurtful and damaging moments later. Statements spoken without much thought achieve the opposite; you want to be heard and instead, you drive people away. Aggression is an enemy to intelligent communication. Therefore, there is a need to interrupt the link between emotions and communication by creating room for a thought process.

Many people find it difficult to think before they speak. You might also occasionally suffer the same problem, particularly in instances when you want to prove to everyone the smart person you believe you are. Just to see where you lie, let's conduct a little test.

Assume you are working on a project that you must submit in two hours and your husband or wife rushes into the room. He or she has been watching television and come across an upcoming story about a politician, let's say, Donald Trump. Apparently, the President tweeted something controversial and it has now gone viral. There is a backlash from the people and the conversation surrounding the issue has been heating up. You already know all that because you were scrolling through your Twitter feed a few minutes before. However, your spouse wants to narrate all the nagging details, from what the president said to what the people said.

Do you wait until your spouse has finished narrating, listening keenly, and then let him know that you had come across something similar on Twitter or do you cut their statement short and alert them on your upcoming deadline? If you will sincerely take the first option, you're good to go. If you're like most of us who will succumb to pressure and take the second option, well, we have a lot to learn.

It is not difficult to let people know that you are smart or are already informed of what is happening. First, take a minute before you speak and ask yourself, "Is anything I will say helpful to the situation? Will it make it better or worse?"

If the answer is negative, move on to the next step where you say, "Thank you for telling me that honey. I actually came across something similar on Twitter." Now, try exercising this level of control in a different situation, making sure to use a person you are used to, like a best friend, and if you pass, you are on the right track.

The minute you allow anger to get between you and reason, you end up looking unwise rather than wise. You are forced to make apologies that can be quite embarrassing. The results of speaking or acting without thinking are not as subtle as we have portrayed; it's just hurting another's feelings and getting away with an apology later. This attitude can cause you to lose your job, break the relationship you have with your children, reputation damage, get you arrested, and other unfavorable life-changing events that can shatter your life.

- Take a Chill Pill (Keeping Your Cool)

Assuming that your speech has been thoughtful, and you have not lashed out at anyone, do not allow the negative emotions to flare up again. You probably still feel like chocking someone, smashing them in the face, or running out of the room, but here's what you should do; take a chill pill. If you have already brought rationality into the picture, allow it to direct the course of what you do next. In the meantime, relax. Keep your cool.

Here are a few steps you can take to help you remain calm:

1. Speak to yourself, convincing your person to calm down. Repeat this and any other gentle phrases like 'you're still fine,' 'it will be okay' or 'nothing will change' and any other phrases you find soothing.
2. Leave the heated environment and go elsewhere. Take a walk, ask for a timeout, or go for a run. Do not come back yet; give it some time.
3. While you are out, visualize things that would calm you down like standing beside the ocean, having a massage, or any other soothing activity.
4. If you feel pressed to do something violent or harmful, start counting from 1 to 20, 50 or 100, until

the feeling passes. This mentally breaks the link between emotion and acting.
5. Use some cold water to wash your hands and face.
6. Slow down on everything and concentrate on your breathing. Breathing consciously involves slow deep breaths that go in through the nose and out through the mouth.
7. Call a friend or a family member you can talk to about the situation
8. Start replacing the negative thoughts you had previously with positive and rational thoughts, and voila! You are calm now. When angry thoughts try to make their way again, remind yourself that becoming angry will not fix a thing.

- Preventing Anger Issues in the Future

You have already won your first battle with anger in a long time and are wondering, what of the next time? Will I successfully deal with strong negative emotions again? What shall I do in the event I do not have a series of steps to follow then? My answer to this is preparation. Prepare now for future encounters. You are likely to succeed when you are prepared than when you are not.

Start by taking time for yourself and use it to release stress. Take up a hobby or an activity for which doing it makes you happy. You could go swimming, chat with your friends, reading a book, or any other that relaxes you and makes you feel good. If you lean towards reading or being with your friends, kindly combine that with a physically involving activity like going to the gym, swimming, or playing a sport because exercise quickly clears the mind too thereby relieving stress.

Some people adopt and practice relaxation techniques like listening to music, yoga, and meditation. Others start journaling their feelings by recording the experience they had, the factors that triggered the anger, and a description of their response. They also record the thoughts that ran through their mind at the time. Keeping a journal and recording these details will help you reflect on your anger management techniques and to establish any pattern there could be.

It also helps to think of all possible outcomes of an outburst. I did this a few months ago when I flipped out on a friend and slapped him. The slap did not offer much relief. It dawned on me that my next move would hurt him badly or land me in the hands of the law and turned away immediately. The next day, while scrolling through YouTube videos, I found prison documentaries in which prisoners are asked to tell their stories. The common denominator in all the stories I hear was that a moment's anger had driven the person to act irrationally. It does not take much to have you behind bars; flared up anger, an irrational thought, and there goes your freedom. This thought has carried me over the last few months and not in a single instance have I acted irrationally.

In the same way, take a moment to ponder on your anger moments. What could they cost you? Your freedom? A relationship with your children? A happy marriage with your awesome husband or wife? Your career? Traumatizing your children? What are you ready to exchange for a moment's 'satisfaction'? When you reflect on these things, you are likely to find that getting angry is not worth it. Take note of the emotions that lead you to anger, and those that you feel when you are angry. Is it confusion, depression, anxiety, or frustration? Take note of this feeling and address it appropriately.

Learn how to communicate well with others, even if it means taking a book from the shelf to learn communication skills or watching those you admire handle stressful situations. Do they speak calmly and rational? Try doing what they do. You will realize so much progress. If you prefer learning in a formal set up, go ahead and register for that class. If you need professional help, go ahead and seek counseling. You are in charge of your boat.

- Looking at the Big Picture

A different way to overcome anger is to focus on other things and not your problems. This is what we call looking for the big picture in a situation. It requires you to explore the good aspects of a situation or a person rather than on the small issue that is bringing negative emotions. For example, if you are angry that your spouse forgot to buy some groceries, consider the fact that he or she honored your request and went to the store. Consider also that the spouse bought some of the items on your list. This is worth appreciation. Let him know that you are grateful.

You could also be stressing over your health. An upset stomach or the flu could be causing you to feel frustrated, helpless, and a tad annoyed. However, you are alive and well, you are not lying on a hospital bed, and you get to have people show their love as they take care of you. You have a lot going for you other than the pain you feel.

This is the bigger picture. It puts into focus the positive things about life ignoring the little specs that bring pain and anger. It helps you develop an attitude of gratitude so that during tough times, not necessarily the angry moments, you can focus on what is going well in your life and realize that many of these problems are molehills and not mountains.

The bigger picture need not rotate around you and your affairs. You can sit down and focus on the offender's circumstances. Take into account the unique challenges the person has had to face in life and take note of possible past unmet needs. It is likely that the person is only reacting to his unique challenges. More than blaming, a person like this will need empathy, and you can try giving it to them, mentally, at least. When you think in this direction, you are sure to feel much better and your anger will neutralize. You will find yourself adapting to this mode of thinking and you will easily control your anger. People will begin looking up to you just as you admire other people around you.

- Switch Your Perspective

Interesting fact — human beings are the only creation that gets to choose how it perceives the world around them. You have the freedom to choose your response to the circumstances of life, and how to perceive what happens to you. If a coworker brushes past you causing you to drop a pile of books, you decide whether she did it on purpose or not, independent of her intentions. However you take it, what you perceive stays in your mind and your heart, and influences your emotions.

Influenced by past unmet needs, most people react based on their old scars and hurt. People with rage, for example, only hear and react to their anger. They see themselves as targets and will use others as targets of their anger too. These people experience selective amnesia at the peak of their anger and when they calm down, many of them cannot even tell what threw them into that rage. They cannot remember what they spoke or did and are often shocked by the violence and harm they cause. Once the incidence has passed, the person is very remorseful.

Without understanding the nature of people with that kind of rage, it may be impossible to separate the person from his actions. Done repeatedly, you would not be blamed for thinking that the person is taking you for a ride. The idea of amnesia in itself makes it less believable. However, once you learn about what the person is going through, you are less likely to get angry after the feat. You could actually begin to explain to him what happens when he becomes extremely angry, and the person will be prompted to seek help. Alternatively, you could become resentful of them and walk away from such a person. It all depends on what you see.

When dealing with a person prone to anger, whether extreme or mild, you get to make the choice between staying with them, understanding them, or letting them go. However, before you make any permanent decision, consider practicing this exercise.

Begin by reminding yourself of an encounter with the person that left you angry, frustrated, and irritated. Do you remember what the person did to provoke these feelings? Why did the person react as he did? Now, try to come up with two plausible explanations for his actions. Think about how each of the explanations makes you feel. Which of the two makes you feel less angry? Pick that one and frame your mind around this idea. Let this be the reason why the person did that. The method is meant to pick the explanation that will produce the least emotional distress.

Looking at another case, imagine a scenario where you call someone to babysit your children as you run off to work. She is running late and so are you, for your job. You realize that your anger is flaring as you clench your fists and pace around the house. Your first assumption could be that the babysitter is taking advantage of you and wants you to pay her for the time they have not worked. A second assumption could be that the babysitter is caught up in traffic or ran into car trouble and is afraid to call you knowing that she has disappointed you.

If you take the first assumption, you will be fuming mad once she arrives and arguing with her could spoil the day for both of you. If you take the second option, you are likely to remain calm, take the apology when she offers it and heads off to work cheerfully. Take the second option; it will produce the least adverse effects.

Now, apply this reasoning in the situation currently aggravating you and you will be calmer about it.

- Be Assertive (Honest and Polite at the Same Time)

    We have discussed techniques and strategies you can take up to work out anger on your end but this does not mean that you should chicken out and take all the blame. Some angry people are wrong and still need to be corrected. As we said earlier, anger is also a genuine feeling that should not be suppressed and should be expressed to indicate your dissatisfaction with the situation as is. Instead of locking your feelings in, consider becoming assertive in your approach.

    Assertiveness is a primary skill in communication. When a person is assertive, he stands up for himself and expresses his opinion truthfully without getting angry. Assertiveness is about expressing your thoughts while maintaining control of your feelings, without letting emotions run high. Communicating this way is more effective than talking while exhibiting all kinds of igneous behavior. It is also the most effective way of ensuring a balanced posture so that everyone gets his or her side heard and the issues resolved.

    When you are displeased with how something is running or how someone is speaking and treating you, it is wiser to try communicating with them about how you are feeling. It is likely that the person is unaware of how it is affecting you. Being assertive, you will be able to express yourself properly and check your emotions intelligently. You will listen and possibly say, "I get what you are saying but if you consider the issue from my point of view, you will see that…"

Assertiveness does not mean that you should be sacked into the individual's emotions; only agree with them if it makes sense to you. Otherwise, stick to your opinion and maintain your position. You are only required to tolerate a different opinion and not to compromise.

It may take a while to develop this skill, but the more you consciously choose to be assertive when dealing with anger, the more the skills will increasingly be engrained in you. It will become a part of your character and you can confidently express your opinion even in heated discussions, without engaging in childish screaming and whining. More importantly, it will earn you respect among your peers.

- Adopt a Type-B Personality

   The differences in our personalities also play a role in how we deal with heavy situations. Type-A persons are competitive, highly stressed, addicted to achievements, and conscious of their status. They love to multi-task, are constantly trying to achieve a goal, are constantly on edge, and are prone to heart conditions and diseases. Type-B personalities are relaxed, laid-back, recognize the social aspect of life, and are able to prioritize. Type-B personalities like to work with others on projects to avoid overburdening themselves, believing that the way to achieve happiness in life is to balance out everything.

   The highly tense inside environment that a Type-A personality has already created makes them quite irritable. They are advised to strive to adopt a number of Type-B tendencies such as:

- *A wider view*: Type-A personalities think in one direction, and one direction only. Their minds focus on work. Type-B personalities, on the other hand, express interest in a number of things beyond their work such as hobbies, spirituality, patriotism, chatting with family and friends, relationships, and nature. Adopting this worldview could help Type-A personalities ease the pressure they put on work and achievement.

- *Relaxing*: Type-A personalities are famous for their sense of agency. Being one, I am always dragging people all over in fear of being late. This person likes to keep time and can be tipped off by lateness, even by minutes. Type-Bs enjoy the flexibility and do not worry about the tasks they will not have accomplished by the end of the day. Taking up this trait could significantly ease the anxiety Type-As feel in traffic jams during rush hour.

- *Considering others not just yourself*: Type-As are not selfish, but they tend to capitalize 'I' in all they do. They hold themselves in high regard and are constantly speaking about their achievements. Type-As are likely to think that all negative comments are directed to them, and will react fast. Type-Bs are humble and do not feel entitled. They are likely to let a negative comment go by even when directed at them. This humble nature would go a long way in helping Type-As lower their ego and irritability.

- *Avoiding competition*: Type-As have numbers on their fingertips, ready to count to you their achievements. It would be easier and more socially accommodating to say, "The year has been productive" instead of running numbers on the number of deals you were a part of. You are more likely to be unhappy and embarrassed when Type-Bs fail to acknowledge these achievements. Instead of focusing on the achievement, Type-As should learn to enjoy the process and the experience.

- *Inquisitive*: Type-B personalities are constantly running around looking to enlarge their horizon in the form of diverse relationships, listening to different viewpoints and life experiences. Type-As should seek to explore life to increase their scope. They should also get to experience the thrills of uncertainty over which Type-Bs thrive.

To that end, Type-As are encouraged to expand their world to reduce the stress they accumulate focusing on one thing only.

Chapter 4: Self-Management for Better Mental Health

Taking steps towards caring for your mental health does not always involve meds and therapy. At its basic, you can also care for your mental wellness by identifying what you desire or need, however small, and then go ahead to meet those needs. It can be as easy as taking a glass of water to go out with friends or going for a run, anything to make your mind relax.

As the world gets busier, you can easily be caught up in beating deadlines at work or meeting the needs of your family that you forget about yourself and your health. Moms and single dads are particularly prone to this. They manage a career, care for the family, and barely get time to themselves. Although they develop resilience as they go, one can easily crack under this mountain of pressure. In a country where one in every four is now suffering from mental health problems, it is time you took your place and care for your mental health.

Below are a number of points that will guide your journey of self-care:

- Stress Management

    Stress is a natural part of life and although some stressors are easy to avoid, such as having a long-distance relationship or joining a sports team, others are difficult to avoid. You only have to find a healthy way to respond to them, beginning from an individual level.

    Prevention should be your first action plan to cut short the buildup of stressors. Begin by taking good care of yourself emotionally, mentally, and physically by feeding properly, exercising, taking some time to relax, and getting an adequate amount of sleep. Instead of having to check numerous items on your list daily, choose to do less to have relaxation time. Prioritize your activities by examining what is of most importance to you today, and in the next 5 years. Set limits to what you can do by turning down some people with a simple 'no' to avoid overworking yourself. It is also important to enjoy the fruits of what you do by setting aside some time and money for fun activities with friends and family.

After blocking the additional stressors' path, focus on relieving the existing stress. Examine what you like to do to take off some pressure. Some people prefer to eat or drink their feelings sitting with a bottle of beer, eating fast foods, or drowning their tears in a bucket of ice cream. While these methods may be effective, how about trying out healthier options like seeking help from a professional or a friend, writing your feelings, changing the environment, or gaming. You could also adopt relaxation techniques like yoga, breathing, and meditation.

If your schedule or the nature of your environment does not allow you to do and the activities listed above, you may need a complete behavior change. Changing how you are and what you do will need considerable effort on your side. However, if you are still intent on following through, start by turning these activities into goals. For example, you can dedicate three hours each week to chat and catch up with friends. You could also set aside ten minutes each day to focus on breathing. These goals should be put down on paper to increase the chance of following them through. Remember to reward positive steps and to ask for help where needed.

- Achieve the Balanced Life

The boundaries between work and a personal life continually thin out, and work could be limiting your personal life. Creating a clear demarcation can be quite difficult especially if your career is quite demanding or that you anticipate changes like layoffs at your place of work. In addition, technology has merged work and home life, creating an instant connection between the two. However, establishing a healthy balance between the two is not impossible; you could apply some strategies to help you restore that balance.

Before we evaluate the process of establishing and reestablishing a work-life balance, it is prudent for us to evaluate what awaits you if you do not take action. A poor work-life relationship will have detrimental effects on you. First, you will end up fatigued and when tired, your productivity automatically lowers negatively affecting your reputation and the chances of you holding that job much longer.

Secondly, there is a chance that you could stretch yourself into poor health. Too much pressure on your body from accumulated stress will, in turn, affect your immune system, making you susceptible to all kinds of diseases. Come to think of it, if you are working, when was the last time you saw the sun and basked in its vitamin D? Do you get time to prepare healthy meals at home? Certainly not.

Thirdly, you lose time that you could have spent bonding with family and friends. If you are constantly working, it is likely that you will miss important milestones and events in the lives of your loved ones. This may harm these relationships and cause you to lose them eventually. Losing these relationships will cause you much pain, sorrow, and regret.

Lastly, the more you give yourself, the more people will expect from you. If you work for more hours, you will be very productive and given more responsibilities that will only make your life more stressful.

To strike a balance between these two important spheres of life, you will need two winning strategies:

o The first is to set limits. Understand that without limits, your obligations will take all your time, without leaving any for a social life. Set limits by doing the following:

1. *Say no sometimes.* No is not disrespectful, it only sets boundaries between what you can and cannot do. It stops you from taking on too much responsibility and gives you time to do what is meaningful to you.
2. *Manage your time more efficiently.* Setting aside time for an activity reduces the frequency of interruptions and prevents one activity from dragging for too long. In addition, you could avoid or delegate the activities that are difficult and those that are draining to focus on tasks that interest you. Only do what is necessary for that day.

3. *Weigh your options.* If you get the opportunity to work flexible hours, work from home, or schedule your hours, take advantage of it. When you have control over when you work, you will be less stressed about it.
4. *Reduce interruptions and shorten the concentration span.* The average person will maintain maximum concentrations for 90 minutes at a time. After that, the level of attention decreases significantly. Interruptions increase the time it takes to finish a task, which means that one task can drag on for a long time thereby creating boredom.
5. *Check your email less often.* The more you check your emails throughout the day, the more you will be distracted from your duties. It will keep you wondering, and you will even try to help others instead of focusing on your own roles.
6. *Have a plan.* A plan lists the things that need to be done and allocates adequate time for each. Have a plan that takes into consideration both phases of life to avoid one phase of your life taking over your entire calendar. Stick to the plan and avoid getting sucked into other people's plans.

- The second strategy for keeping a healthy work-life balance is to begin to take care of yourself better. When you maintain a healthy lifestyle, you are able to cope with stress better. A healthy lifestyle will require you to sleep adequately, eat healthy foods, and set aside some time for relaxation and fun. A support system in the form of family and friends is also essential because they cover you in times of need and crises. Some will also help with daily tasks so that you do not have to do everything yourself.

While it is possible to re-strategize and re-organize your life on your own, it helps to seek professional counsel sometimes. For example, everything may look equally important to you and you may be unable to set priorities. However, a professional will be able to look at each activity objectively and help you gain perspective on what to do. You may be prioritizing taking your child to see the dentist at the expense of a board meeting or prioritizing a board meeting instead of attending your child's first football game. You could have your spouse take your child to the dentist while you make effort to be present during one of your child's most significant events such as his first game. You only need to determine what is of most importance at a time, and a professional could help you weigh each option.

Striking a healthy balance in life is a process and not a one-day event. It goes on for the rest of your life but changes as your interests, your work, and your family life changes. You only need to examine what you prioritize occasionally and to make the right adjustments.

Why Is a Good Sleep Important for Anger Management?

Sleep on it. Many of us have heard this advice more times than we can count. It does not make sense when you think about it keenly. How are you to make a decision while asleep? Turns out that this is not one of the old wives tales, sleeping does indeed help to make better decisions. Research shows that sleep influences retention, emotions, decision-making, mood, and anger, among others.

While you sleep, your mind and body are fast at work. The body takes the opportunity to clear toxins, take out wastes, balance hormones, and repair tissues. This process is complex and requires adequate time to complete. Therefore, when interrupted, it interferes with your temperament, memory, emotional regulation, and response.

When your mood and emotions are right, you are likely to take time to assess the situation deeper and to give a reasonable response. You probably heard a parent say that their child who was throwing a tantrum needed a nap to calm down. This is true because sleeping will help the mind re-evaluate its emotional processing of the situation at hand.

Your memory is key to your decision-making ability because you rely on the past or what you have learned to weigh out merits and demerits. Sleep determines how memories are stored and retrieved in the brain. It also influences the accuracy with which you remember events. Therefore, when you sleep adequately, you are likely to make good decisions and to be happy with the results.

Researchers say that sleep-deprived people tend to make unethical decisions. Sleepy people at work are likely to be sloppy and inefficient, behave defiantly, be rude to others, and intentionally reduce their productivity. This is thought to be largely because the lack of sleep deprives them of the ability to control themselves. It is also thought that glucose levels at the frontal lobe could be depleted, affecting the ability to make decisions and think complex thoughts.

All these factors make a strong case for why you need to value your hours of sleep. A regular sleeping schedule, proper nutrition, exercise, and taking time off are all you need to function optimally. You will enjoy a balanced emotional state that will help you make good decisions and maintain healthy relationships.

If you encounter an emotionally charged situation, take some time to rest. You only need to clear your mind actively with some meditation or breathing to avoid the events of the day tempering with your rest. When you wake up, you will have a changed attitude and perspective.

Best Routines and Tips for Better Sleep

It is difficult to get a good night's sleep while you are still tossing at 3 AM in the morning. Many people become weary in the evening anticipating the agony they will have in the night as they helplessly try to catch some sleep. Some result to medication to ease the process. The truth is that you are not as helpless as you may think. You determine the quality of sleep you get. Just like how the feeling you have when you wake up determines the quality of your day, so do the activities of the day determine the quality of sleep you get.

When you go looking into information about sleep and sleep habits, it is likely that you will find many sources advocating for 'sleep hygiene'. This term is used to refer to the healthy sleeping habits that are meant to help you fall asleep undistracted. These habits are recommended for the treatment of persons suffering from prolonged insomnia during cognitive behavioral therapy. Sleep hygiene enables you to relax and gain control over thoughts that traditionally prevent you from sleeping well.

Below is a description of the practices and techniques to help you achieve sleep hygiene.

- Align Yourself with Your Body's Sleep and Waking up Cycle

    Keeping up with the body's natural sleep and waking up cycle helps you sleep better. If you stick to a regular schedule, you will feel more bouts of energy and refreshment compared to when you sleep intermittently. Begin by setting and sticking to a regular sleep and waking up schedule daily. This helps the body to set its internal clock and readjust itself to enhance the quality of sleep. Choose a time when you are the most tired in order to cut out the tossing and turning. If the schedule allows you enough sleeping time, you should be awake even without an alarm. If you find yourself still needing the alarm, try sleeping earlier.

    Do not allow yourself to get drowsy after a meal. If you feel sleep setting in, do something distracting like cleaning dishes to avoid sleeping before bedtime and having to wake up later in the night. You may also want to limit your napping during the day. Napping may make sleeping at night increasingly difficult. However, if you really need one, limit it to 15-20 minutes only early in the afternoon. In addition, avoid sleeping in during the weekends because when sleeping schedules clash, your symptoms may get worse. Instead, opt for a nap during the day.

- Watch Your Food

    Just as you expected, your meals determine how you sleep, particularly those taken just before bedtime. You must have had to stay up sometime because of an upset stomach or discomfort. When you eat, avoid heavy large meals at night, but eat your dinner early avoiding spicy food that can cause you heartburn in the night. Keep off alcohol because it distracts your sleep cycle. Limit your nicotine and caffeine intake during the day as their effects last even up to twelve hours after consumption. Cut back on refined carbs and sugars also because the energy in them can spring you back to consciousness even in deep sleep. Lastly, avoid drinking too many fluids to reduce bathroom visits in the night.

- Your Sleep Environment Should Matter

    Although a bedtime routine allows your body to relax in readiness for sleep, even the slightest environment changes could affect your sleep. Your room needs to be quiet, dark, cool and ventilated. The bed should be comfortable, with clean bedding that allows you to turn and stretch without getting entangled. Maintain silence and when you cannot eliminate noise from outside, use earplugs to avoid distraction. Ensure that you reserve your bed for sex and sleeping only, and keep away all work, study items, and gadgets.

- Silence Your Mind

    Make effort to avoid dragging any residual anger, stress, and worry to bed because they keep your brain from unwinding and seeking fresh inspiration.

- Get Back Your Sleep

In the event you wake up in the night and have trouble getting back to sleep, the following tips could help you overcome sleeplessness.

1. *Avoid thinking about it*: If you start stressing the fact that you are unable to sleep, you only influence your brain to stay alert. Instead, breathe and focus on how your body responds. Breathe in slowly and out slowly. Repeat this exercise and feel your body relaxing again.

2. *Focus on relaxation, not sleep*: While you may be trying to sleep, anxiety will only keep you from sleeping. Meditate and visualize your body relaxed and in complete rest. Relaxation is also good since it rejuvenates the body just as sleep does.

3. *Do something quiet and non-stimulating*: If you still cannot sleep, it may be time to get out of your bed and do something worthwhile, at least. Ideally, take a book and read it under dim lights. Avoid screens because they would signal to the brain that it is waking time.

4. *Put it down on paper*: If you roused from your sleep worried about something or a new idea came to your mind, take a paper and pen it down; you will worry about it the next day. Drift back to sleep knowing that a good sleep will charge you to deal with the hustles of the next day.

Transform Your Anger into Constructive Action

Children in pain or frustrated from not having their way lose it sometimes. They roll on the ground, jump up and down, yell and cry their tears out. Parents call it tantrums, a hissy fit, a melt-down and a whole load of names. You may have seen it at home, school, or at the mall. However, as a teenager, a young adult or an adult, you cannot start rolling because you are upset. You are expected to have mastered the art of channeling your anger and fury into constructive activities. Parents teach us from an early age.

Despite the high expectations on an adult, emotions will occasionally overwhelm you. There are new situations and stimuli every day that you are not equipped to deal with. This is the reason many people are still trying to get a hold of anger management techniques. One of the most effective ones is to channel that anger into something else. Anger is a form of energy, and since you cannot destroy energy, you can transform it into something useful just as lightning can be channeled into power.

To channel anger is to direct the energy you feel towards a worthwhile task so that you are able to keep that energy away from your mind and emotions. The task to which you are directing energy should always be positive. Otherwise, you will become destructive, driven by your anger. For example, you can go for a run and do an extra mile, read and respond to countless unread emails, or complete that task that you have postponed time and again. Only ensure that what you engage in is productive.

Some people use channeled anger to make plans. Angry people

are determined. They are looking for revenge and they want it now. They demand success. In the spirit of determination, they can turn this rage into a business plan, a savings plan, and any other idea that will benefit them in the future.

I have seen someone turn his anger into a cab business. My friend's father called for a cab to take him to a meeting with investors he believed would change his life instantly. He had dreamt of starting a restaurant but whenever he made steps to execute his idea, everything came tumbling down. He arrived late and the investors were not impressed, especially because he arrived an hour late. Frustrated by the cab driver, my friend's father sat down on a bench in the park and drew a plan for what would be a successful cab business. His anger birthed the career that transformed his life. He does not recall his restaurant ideas. You too can transform an unpleasant experience into an amazing idea that will change your life and change the world.

After drawing up a plan, do not forget to execute it. What is a thought or a plan without execution? As soon as you have a plan down on paper, begin to execute it. Do the things you intended to do while you still have the energy and the will to do them. Take advantage of that wave of determination and begin to catapult yourself to success systematically.

Many people begin to doubt themselves at this stage. They become contemplative and allow the doubts to flood their minds, interrupting the course of action. Some people begin to doubt their abilities while others wonder what people will think. It is the reason many talented writers having manuscripts collecting dust in their drawers. They were afraid to take them for publishing fearing rejection. It is also the reason others have not started their dream business wondering what society will think of them if they become entrepreneurs instead of focusing solely on children. It is also the reason others have not submitted their college application papers. In truth, we all have things we did not do because we allowed our fears and thoughts to get in the way.

To avoid this delay, move now in the spirit of your channeled energy. Do not stop to think, do not second-guess yourself. These days, whenever a thought that could potentially stop me comes, I stop and ask myself, "What worst could happen?" If I submit my manuscript, the worst that could happen is the publishers sending me away. So what? There are other publishing houses.

Begin to ask yourself the same question. What worst could happen if you sent in your application to that college you desire to attend? At best, they will take you. Worst case scenario, they will reject your application. Pat yourself on the back either way. You made an effort.

If you are yet to observe this, allow me to share with you what I have. 9 out of 10 times, people reward effort and not performance. A person can have talent and do nothing about it while another can keep making effort and succeed. It is said that persistence breaks resistance.

Let us try to get this into perspective. Pretend that you are an investor or a sponsor of a kind. Whenever you hesitate to do something because you fear failure, ask yourself, "If I were an investor, who would I invest in? A person who tried to do something once and succeeded immediately or the one that doing something many times before succeeding?"

While succeeding in the first attempt shows ability and

competence, making several attempts communicates desire, passion, determination, drive, and a desire to know. You would most certainly pick the second candidate. Therefore, keep trying. Keep making effort to succeed and one day, your efforts shall bear fruit.

Although you may want to implement your strategy very fast, it is still wise to double-check to ensure that there are no mistakes. Sometimes, doing things in a rush can lead to failure. For example, if you plan to open a restaurant, check to confirm you have the right premise. Review also the outlay of your plans to ensure that they are right so that adrenaline does not lead you to do things you wouldn't do.

In conclusion, let anger be the rocket fuel that drives you out of your comfort zone into success realms you never thought you would achieve.

Into Practicing Fitness

Talking of ways to channel built-in rage, how about delving into the world of physical activity? Experts speak of a strong correlation between emotional health and exercise. They recommend it for managing stress, anger, and rage. When you exercise while driven by these strong emotions, you are able to kick harder, run longer, and jump higher than you do when in a peaceful state. Experts recommend running, weight-lifting, boxing, and HIIT.

If the high-energy exercises are not for you, opt for aerobics. Do 3 sets of triceps extensions, bicep curls, and side raises, ten at a time. Focus on the contracting muscles and let your rage be felt there.

If you are down and sad, it is better to exercise as a group. Being around people, even strangers could cheer you up. Group workouts are known to produce endorphins, the feel-good hormone that lifts your spirits. Do anything to return to your cheerful self.

Into a New Hobby

Anger and rage can also be channeled into a hobby. Below are a number of creative hobbies you can take up to calm down.

- Gardening

    After working all day seven or six days a week, it is easy to feel like an alien when you go outside. You lose all connection that you had with the outside world. However, there is a genius way to regain this connection and that is through gardening. Scientists say that this hobby is perfect for lifting your spirits when you feel stressed and angry.

    A study in the Netherlands subjected a group of people to a strenuous and stressful task and on completing asked them to split into two groups, each choosing between gardening and reading to lower their stress levels. At the end of the exercise, subjects who chose gardening were found to be in a better mood than those who chose reading proving that gardening is an effective stress-reliever.

    Gardening is made effective not only by the feel of nature as you interact with the soil but also by a bacteria living in the dirt. Evidence shows that the ground hosts a bacterium called *Mycobacterium vaccae* which is known to cheer people up. This harmless bacterium boosts the production of serotonin which enhances the mood. People who are exposed to the bacteria from childhood are also reported to have a healthy immune system when older. It just might be of benefit for you to play in the dirt.

- Painting and Drawing

    This is one hobby known to help people overcome their trauma and stress. Therapists use it to treat psychological distress from domestic abuse, emotional trauma, depression, physical abuse, anxiety, and other psychological problems. Prison inmates who draw are said to have a positive mood change that helps them to gain a locus of control. However, even without professional direction, you can reap the benefits of this hobby.

    When you sculpture, draw, or paint, your brain produces dopamine that activates the body's reward system. This system is known to increase creativity and lower distractions like stress and self-doubt. Therefore, when you engage in any of these activities, you feel pleasure, ownership, and freedom.

- Photography

    Photography is a hobby that anyone can pick up, unlike other creative hobbies that require some talent. You only use a camera lens to capture existing beauty, without having to create anything. The beauty of photography is that it teaches you to see evident beauty and that which is not so evident. Photography changes your worldview. You begin to view things from multiple angles, most of which other people would not see. You also get to notice what you would overlook normally.

The effect of seeing beauty in everything is that you become happier, fulfilled, and satisfied. However, there is a learning curve involved.

Chapter 5: Tips to Handle a Partner with Anger Issues

While you may know how to manage your anger and channel it to productive causes, these techniques do not work when you are calm and dealing with an angry person. This is a whole other ball game. You will need to remain calm and help them work through their emotions carefully to avoid their contagious negative energy rubbing up on you.

Dealing with an angry partner is particularly difficult because it involves a combination of volatile emotions like love, anger, jealousy, and frustration among others that erupts fast. It is also a challenge because if the anger bursts are occasional, you may find yourself resenting the person or developing another character that is not you. You may also be tempted to change them, which often works against you.

Here's how to deal with an angry partner without going nuts!

Maintain Your Cool

When your partner is lashing at you and possibly making unfounded statements, the one thing you want to do is to lash back at them, defend yourself, and expose them for the liars they truly are. This is not a wise thing to do. When you consciously choose to remain calm, your partner will get over his or her emotions quicker and then you can reason out together.

Keeping calm is only a strategy to keep things from spilling over, however, it does not eliminate the fact that both of you are angry. It comes from a mature realization that you will not achieve anything if both of you are screaming at each other.

The issue at hand should wait until both of you are sober-minded and calm.

Keeping your cool also means that you do not get to sit and mimic their reactions, make faces or acting withdrawn. Either of these will only add heat to an already messy situation because body language communicates as effectively as verbal communication. Instead, nod and only give a brief verbal response where needed. The brief response should be something like, "I hear you" rather than raise your concerns or insulting them saying, "How dumb can you be." Vicious statements like these will only get you into trouble and make it even more difficult for the partner to calm down.

If you do not understand a point the partner is making, respectfully and calmly ask for more details. That way, the person will feel that he or she is heard. In explaining to you their concerns, they may also get a chance to re-evaluate the reason for letting their emotions flare up as such. It helps to remain warm to the side of this person that you like. Focus on that in your mind. Remind yourself that you love him or her and that the anger shall pass.

Identify the Triggers

Anger is birthed by pain and hurt, and when a person is angry, he is only trying to manifest that pain. When a partner is angry at you, it does not automatically mean that you hurt them. People sometimes take out their emotions on the softest and safest target. Not to mean that you are out of the equation; it could be that you opened old wounds of his past unmet needs with something you said or did.

Just to help the men, it could be that the anger your girlfriend is projecting towards you for not buying her a gift is rooted in the fact that you are yet to propose. Ladies are deeply hurt when the man is not showing any signs of commitment, making them question the entire relationship. Or, she could also be hurting from the memories of something that happened to her a long time ago. Or, she may be hurting from something that happened in her personal life like losing a job.

Many times, it is difficult to point directly at the reason a person is angry, which makes keeping calm and listening to them quite sensible. When you listen to them, you are able to filter out the anger trigger under all that mile of emotion. Many times or half the time, the anger will have nothing to do with you or your relationship. It could be from other areas in your partner's life spinning out of control.

Communicate in a Productive Manner

Once both parties calm down, agree on a set time to address the anger and the issues underlying. Be gentle when speaking about the emotions your partner expressed and how they made you feel. This is not meant to help you play victim but to show him or her that the issues also affect you.

Talking about the issues should not provide an opportunity for you to rant and present a list of your partner's failures. If you believe that your partner is lying or has ludicrous ideas, which you possibly already do, do not say it aloud. Allow them to vent out unashamedly because it creates a safe environment for self-expression. This is particularly important for men because many of them fear opening up to talk about their feelings. It also maintains his dignity because he will feel that even the least of his feelings matter to you.

Ask questions to help you understand the situation better and to help your partner connect the dots better. For example, ask "Why does that make you feel..." or "How does that influence this?" In asking these questions, you will realize that you were at fault or your partner will realize that he or she has blown the situation out of proportion. Either way, work towards protecting each party's pride and developing a self-correct attitude for the sake of your relationship.

In case you realize that indeed you contributed to your partner's anger or helped to open old wounds and hurts, apologize sincerely. Even when what you did feels trivial to you, realize that it was significant enough to cause him or her to go off. However, only apologize for what you did because it will be more hurtful if your partner realizes that you only apologized so the issue can rest. Kindly note that you are also responsible for how your partner perceives your actions. If you did something and unintentionally hurt your partner, apologize for that too. However, if you are not responsible for the hurt, do not apologize for it. For example, if your partner misplaced his car keys, say "Sorry that you misplaced your keys" and do not take the blame for it.

Choose Your Battles

You probably heard the phrase 'pick your battles' in a number of settings. This phrase originated from the military in reference to their combat activities. When they picked their battles, they lost some fights, but the mission was to win the war. This simply means that you should not waste your emotional resources, time, or energy engaging in a battle you will certainly not win.

People have and are entitled to their beliefs, preferences, expectations, and opinions, which can make the relationship a battlefield when either side is not willing to bow. Religion and political differences effectively create this kind of environment and it is best to exercise restraint on your part, at least. While you can talk and argue with your partner about anything, it is best to be selective and let go, reserving your energy only for that which fosters peace and matters. If you insist on fighting over everything, you may end up winning the arguments but at the expense of your relationship.

Exercise Patience

Most certainly, resolving the issue at hand will not magically wand off your partner's anger issues. It may take years before your partner is able to overcome the pain, the fear and the helplessness he or she feels. In another instance, your partner will yet again use anger to shield his or her inner feelings and to gain a sense of control. This is the reason it is important to understand the underlying issue so that the occasional outbursts do not make you resentful of them. What will hold you down is your conscious and consistent intentions to work on your relationship and help your partner through the process. Be patient as he or she makes effort to detach from the underlying factors and in due time, your investment will pay.

Empathize

When you have understood what your spouse is going through, you are able to show empathy even if the person is not able to open up and you are sure that something significant is bothering him, making him scared or embarrassed to speak up. Other times, the angry party cannot even tell where the anger is coming from. Whatever the reason, you love your partner and it hurts you when he or she is hurting. Empathize.
Here's how to empathize. First, pray. I have found prayer to be

an effective tool towards understanding the pain of others. It gets you to the point of admitting that you are powerless too, and cannot resolve the issue yourself; you need a higher power. It reminds you to view your spouse through a humane lens, realizing that your partner is also prone to mistakes and weaknesses. This attitude will soften your heart and melt any resentment you have towards your spouse. Prayer allows you to ask God for joy, peace, endurance, and the motivation you need to press on.

The second step towards empathy is becoming a safe place for your partner even when he or she does not reciprocate. This step is quite difficult. It demands unconditional love without the assurance of receiving the same in the future. However, if you assure your partner that you can a safe space, he or she will open up. The walls he or she uses to shield and hide will fall and the relationship will transform for the better.

The third step in showing empathy is to be consistent in giving it. Consistency in relationships is key to establishing confidence and trust. If you become a safe space for your partner today, ensure that you do not use his or her weaknesses against them tomorrow. Your partner will have difficulty trusting you in the future and the anger can only get worse because he or she does not have anyone to share with. Of course, there will be days when you are angry and vindictive towards one another, but maintain consistency in presenting love and acceptance.

Empathy will indeed bring the two of you closer and save your relationship.

Be Respectful and Firm

For any relationship to work, boundaries must be set. They govern and clearly demarcate the difference between personal space, personal interests, principles, and values, and that which is shared with a partner. However, just as 'rules are meant to be broken,' your partner, especially one prone to anger, will try to shift them occasionally. Some of the shifts are done unintentionally while in others, the partner intends to test how far he or she can go (I have tried that myself).

Anger should not be an excuse for any reckless behavior. Let your partner know that whichever state he or she is in, your boundaries must be respected. Make a decision on what you can tolerate and what you cannot stand, then bring it to the partner's knowledge. They may insist on shifting the boundary lines, still, be firm about what you mean, but do it respectfully. These boundaries are not born out of selfishness. Instead, they help to cultivate mutual respect.

In the event that a partner crosses a line when he or she flares up, bring it up in the talk you have when he or she calms down. Clearly indicate the boundary your partner crossed, how you felt, and what the consequences of your partner doing so are. For example, if you do not tolerate body shaming, you may say, "I do not appreciate that you spoke about my height in a manner to pull me down or intimidate me. It made me feel small and looked down upon. I am unwilling to be with a person who brings me down every instance he gets, blaming it on the anger."

In this statement, you will have indicated that he crossed the line by speaking negatively about your height, that it made you feel insignificant, and that you are unwilling to tolerate a partner that puts you down whenever he is angry. Saying that you are unwilling to tolerate body shaming does not mean that you will be walking out on the relationship, it gives him the opportunity to shape up or ship out. In all honesty, being in a relationship with someone that makes you feel insignificant and small is unhealthy.

Seek Influence Rather Than Control

Avoid making effort to change your partner. It will get you no results. Instead, seek to influence him by showing him the positives of your position. Just like mentoring, influence is gradual. It shifts your focus from what your partner is doing or thinking wrong and you begin to focus on being on your best behavior so that the partner begins to learn from you.

For example, if your partner lashes out when in anger, avoid lashing out when he makes you angry. Be calm and gentle even where you feel an angry reaction is deserved. It is likely that your partner will notice it and when he gets angry the next time, he will begin to show some level of control in how he expresses his emotion. Slowly, you will begin to win the partner to your side.

There is an expression that suggests that you can catch more flies with honey than vinegar. This expression illustrates the concept of influence over control. Sweetness is able to pull an individual to your side better than beating their head down and dragging them around. Have you heard people say that you are the average of five people you are closest to and that bad company ruins good morals? These phrases revolve around the power of influence. I hear my friends saying control breeds resistance, which could be true. There is an innate desire to go against the grain sometime, and being asked to conform to your partner's ideology might be one.

Therefore, in instances where you desire positive outcomes, lean toward influence. It is gradual but effective.

Do Not Put up with Insulting and Disrespectful Behavior

There is not a reason in the world that sufficiently explains why you should put up with disrespect and bad behavior to maintain a relationship. If your partner treats you with disrespect or by his actions you read that the problem is only escalating, set or strengthen your boundaries. Let your partner know what you can and cannot accept in the relationship and emphasize that you will leave if the boundaries are crossed.

Your boundaries should not deter you from noticing red flags either. Almost all domestic abuse incidences start with a demonstration of anger by either throwing or breaking things, shouting, acting out in public, physical aggression, verbal abuse, and any other sign that potentially frightens you. Once the partner begins to show any of these signs, take precaution and leave the room. In addition, rather than dealing with similar incidences for the rest of your life, consider leaving for good.

Walk Away

It is difficult to be the one that picks the pieces of your relationship repeatedly. Relationships are meant to be two-way and if you are the one that constantly fights for it, it is only right for you to try something different. Some people have a dismissive and condescending attitude, and will not change their minds even when you go to great lengths to influence them positively. Sometimes, the company your partner keeps could be the problem and if you are fighting to influence him against the influence of his five buddies, you are fighting a losing battle.

Walking away is as good for you as it is for him. For example, you shouldn't have to accommodate verbal abuse because it could lead to hurt and abuse that will affect your current and future relationships. Women are particularly good at remembering what someone said. Therefore, if a person insults or body shames you during one of his outbursts, it is likely that you will remember the insult for the rest of your life. A man whose ego is wounded by words or actions will also take time to overcome this hurt if he ever does. This is the reason many people's self-esteem lowers in relationships.

If you feel like the situation will not change, walk away, to save both of you. It will save you from emotional trauma and the possibility of abuse. It will give your partner the opportunity to grow up and learn to respect personal boundaries. Hopefully, your partner will have learned a lesson and behave better in their next relationship. In addition, this loss could push your partner to seek professional help.

Chapter 6: Dealing with Children and Family Members with Anger Issues

Children are little bundles of joy, but as they grow up, this joy can turn into frustration especially if the child has anger issues. It is difficult to know where to begin when handling an angry child. Some children also have a lot of anger pent up in them and will yell and become aggressive at the slightest provocation. Fits like these can leave parents, guardians, caregivers, and teachers wondering what to do.

Angry family members can pose a challenge too when dealing with them. It is possible that you do not know enough about them to come up with an origin for their pain. For example, it is likely that you do not know everything that has happened in your parent's life from birth, and sometimes, even a sibling will surprise you. It is important to learn how to handle their anger and pain, being careful to show respect for their individual life journeys.

A Child with Anger Issues

When dealing with a child, beware that the child is watching you. The manner in which you handle your own or the child's anger sets the precedence for how the child handles anger for the rest of his or her life unless otherwise influenced. It determines how the two of you will handle subsequent disappointments and frustrations. If you do not want to have to deal with tantrums in the future, work on it today.

Here are some tips to help you deal with an angry child.

Set Lower Expectations

When dealing with children, make certain to factor in their ages. A child does not have the knowledge resources you have, the experience you have had, or know how to control emotions like you have learned have and practiced over the years. A child is only now learning about life. The little they know is what you have taught them and what they have been exposed to in their environment around them.

A child also magnifies small things. Their little mind is yet to understand causal links between events. I once watched a child cry uncontrollably because he had dropped a pen and did not know how to get it back from the ground. I thought to myself, "It only takes bending and picking it up," but this child did not know this. He possibly thought that it is the worst thing that could happen in life. When dealing with a child, whether two or ten years old, remember that their understanding is limited. Do not rush the process; let them grow their understanding a little bit at a time.

A child is also said to be the book in which parents and other adults inscribe indelibly their beliefs, values, and morals. Everything that happens to them is a learning process. Do not get angry when your child shouts at you; do not expect him to know that he should respect his elders. Where could he have learned it from anyway? Calm down and explain social values to them and just as it takes practice to know algebra, it will take firm and repeated teaching for the child to conform to your ways.

Validate Emotions

As a parent, guardian, caregiver, or any other adult taking care of a child, it is important to value the child's emotions. If the child cries, do not start rebuking the child or demanding that they stop crying. Rather, validate what the child is feeling. Say, "I know you are hurting so much; in your position, I would be crying too." A reply like this will make you look like a friend, you will not be the target for all the anger and anxiety the child feels. It is also likely that the child will open up to you more.

When you become a friend, the child will trust you because they feel that you are on their side, whether it is the right or wrong one. For example, if the child is angry at you and says that he or she does not want to see you and demands to be left alone, do so but assure the child that you love him or her and will be available if they want to talk. Let the child feel your support even in those tense moments.

Establishing trust also lets the child know that you trust their ability to process emotions properly, soaring his or her confidence.

Validation is also key to calming the child down. If you assure the child that you understand his or her feelings, it is unlikely that he or she shall respond in a defensive angry manner. When you acknowledge the child's feelings, his or her anger softens and the child is able to create room for learning how to cope and to empathize. If, on the other hand, you disregard these feelings, the child will fight to defend his or her sense of self.

Differentiate Emotion and Behavior

Kids do not know how to distinguish between anger and aggressive behavior. At least, from what has been modeled in real life and on TV, an angry person speaks violently, throws stuff around and will even hurt others. However, take the time and patiently teach your child how to label his or her feelings. Make the child verbalize them by using terms like disappointed, angry, irritated, frustrated and other like terms.

A child should understand that angry feelings are allowed, but aggressive behavior is wrong. You may say, "It is okay to be angry that your brother took the remote control, but it is not okay to yell at him." Help the child see that distinction. You will be surprised when the child comes to report to you when the brother takes the remote instead of crying or yelling. This is a positive response; ensure that you reward it.

Sometimes, the child will not be able to verbalize feelings only because he or she does not recognize them. To increase the child's knowledge of them, begin to talk about it and describe the feelings in simple language. Over time, the child will begin to describe these feelings better and this will enhance communication and understanding.

Exercise Patience

Patience is an incredibly valuable quality when dealing with children, one of the reasons being that you need to control yourself and the second being that you need to be more accommodating of their learning processes. One of the values many parents desire if you ask them is to be more patient with their children. They desire not to yell or curse when they have to repeat the same instructions time and again. They also desire to remain calm when their child is venting.

As an adult, you set the pace for how children in your household or under your care behave and to do this effectively, you may want to take some valuable steps. First, identify what triggers you to anger and take note of when and where this happens most times. For example, some people tend to lose their cool in the morning when they need to get to work or in the evening when they are tired or disappointed at what they find at home. Being in a hurry, tired, or disappointed will cause you to flare up fast at the slightest irritation. Once you have taken note of that, move on to work on your response.

Carefully observe what you do when prompted to anger. Observe how your body reacts. Does your heart beat faster, does it become difficult to breathe, or do your palms sweat? What thoughts creep up your mind as you listen to the child talk back? What response do you give? All these questions provide answers that will get you to understand your tipping point.

Just like when dealing with personal anger, come up with a plan of action that details what to do when the anger sets in. For example, you can use the time between getting from work to home to cool down and come up with an action plan of what you will do if you find that your expectations are not met. Also, plan on what to do in the heat of the moment like stepping away or breathing consciously to calm down. Plan also for what will follow once the emotions have cooled down. You could choose to sit by yourself to review the situation or sit with your child to discuss problem-solving methods.

With these steps, you will increasingly be calm in the face of provocation and be able to act rationally in front of your children. It will also give them the opportunity to learn and grow at their own pace without causing you multiple headaches.

Be Firm but Polite

Experts have taught on the need to be both kind and firm when dealing with children. Kindness shows the kid that you respect him or her as a person, while firmness shows the need to respect you. It also shows the seriousness of the situation. Both positive attributes are necessary to promote discipline and respect.

Many adults struggle with this truth fearing that they will become too permissive and accommodating of bad behavior. Others mistake kindness for pleasing the children or rushing to protect and rescue them from life's struggles and disappointments. However, kindness means respecting yourself and the child and validating each party's feelings. You are not kind when you condone disrespect from a child.

For example, if a child is yelling and hurling insults at you, the respectful thing to do is to walk out. This is quite controversial but you will see the reason behind it. Walking away is respecting yourself and not allowing the child to demean you. It actually sets a strong precedence for the child. Otherwise, you will engage in a yelling match or even find yourself becoming violent. Both of you have a better chance of calming down and discussing the matter later while in separate rooms. If you feel the need to take authority in this situation, send the kid to his room, which works too.

On the issue of firmness, the adult sets the rules, period. Adults are also responsible for enforcing them with lectures, boundaries, and punishments. However, this often invites power struggles. Therefore, instead of making it a solo activity, invite your kids to the table and discuss rules pertaining to anger management, among others. Talk about the rules, reasons for having rules, and each party's responsibility in keeping them.

To end, firmness and kindness create an environment of mutual understanding where everyone knows that they are valued and respected and that there is bound to be consequences if they do not reciprocate.

Take Extra Effort to Explain Their Emotions to Them

Children have a right to knowledge, especially concerning that which directly affects them and their feelings. They need to know that every feeling has an origin and that while some originate from good things, others like anger do not originate from good things. Explain to them that when anger comes about, it comes on as a strong feeling that seeks to take complete control but if you are cautious and diligent, you can control the extent to which it flares up.

Explain to them also that everyone experiences anger and that it is part of our natural feelings. Tell the child that anger comes because of fear, disappointment, hurt, loss, unfair treatment, and other negative things that all people suffer. Also demonstrate that when a person is angry, jaws feel tight, feet get cold or hot, muscles tighten, your stomach feels sick, you cry, scream, and may even feel like hurting others or themselves.

Teach the child how people look like when they are angry.

Their faces look red, they become clumsy and walk fast, they bang things, their eyes water, the nose and mouth become pale, and the nostrils get wider. Explain any other signs that your child would recognize. Teach the child that anger can also be good if channeled into productive activities and give them ideas on what to do when angry instead of engaging in destructive things

It is said that information is power. With this knowledge, the child will be able to recognize when he, you, and other people are angry, and behave appropriately.

Acknowledge the Triggers and Drivers to Anger

Keenly observe the child to take note of situations, events, and circumstances that infuriate the child. At this stage, many things will irritate a child, but soon, a trend will emerge. Help the child avoid these triggers to get a handle of the situation and if avoiding them proves impossible, let your child understand them. Knowledge will help the child calm down.

If the child is grown and can monitor his emotions, he can manage them as well. Once the child understands the emotions that cause him to be angry, he can recognize them as they set in, take charge, and manage them before the emotions flare up.

Therapists recommend using art like painting, writing, and drawing to bring emotions to consciousness. These are excellent ways for children unable to recognize and verbalize their emotions to express what is disturbing them. Commend them for making an effort and encourage them to do it more often. It is also important to ask the child to explain the drawing, painting or writing, even when you can clearly see what it is. It helps teachers encourage them to verbalize emotions rather than relying on art all the time. This will make it easier for the child to develop a social life now and later in life.

Develop an Aggression Meter

Many families come up with rules that differentiate between acceptable and unacceptable behavior in expressing anger emotions. While some do not condone raising voices or slamming doors, others give room for such behavior. However, it is always better to avoid behavior like this to prepare your child to live with others in the future.

Setting clear standards means that while you may want to validate the child's feelings, ensure you do not make it seem like you are accepting of the bad behavior. Many of the rules of engagement set do not condone breaking stuff, showing disrespect, hitting others, and throwing things. In setting these rules, involve the children so that they are aware of the consequences of what they do. Children respond more positively to rules they help set.

The aggression meter should work for you too. Some parents lose it and get physical with their children. It could be a shove, a slap, a kick or an insult. Most times than not, the child retaliates and the fight escalates. While we may pretend that all of us are in control of their emotions, the truth is a number of us fail to do so sometimes. If you get caught in one of these, humble yourself and apologize. Say, "I apologize for losing control and shoving you." Only that. Do not start explaining to the child how his actions led you to do that, you want to teach responsibility and genuinely making amends, not excuses.

Adopt Negative Punishment (Time-Out) Instead of Positive Punishment

When a child breaks the anger rules in the house, it is only right if they receive punishment for their actions. Punishment is meant to decrease the probability of repeating undesired behavior and is often delivered immediately. Experts recommend negative punishment over positive punishment.

Negative punishment is that which happens when a desired item or incentive is taken away once the undesired behavior is presented. A child that enjoys swimming can be sent to detention as the rest take the swim class if they misbehave. A child that loves pancakes for breakfast can be forced to take something else for lashing out at his parent. If siblings start fighting over who gets to play a game first, the parent should take away the game altogether.

Positive punishment also presents a negative consequence for bad behavior but in a different way. A child who lashes out at his parents for not finding his favorite toy will be lectured on how to keep his toys properly. A child that breaks things when angry will be asked to collect the fragments as punishment. While both methods aim to lessen undesired behavior, the negative punishment strategy is clear about the negative consequences and reinforces the lesson better than the positive punishment method.

Be careful to punish behavior only, not anger. As long as the child is not breaking any rules, let him be. They too have a right to be angry. For example, if the child begins to swear at you in his outburst, make it clear that the consequence is meant to punish him for swearing. However, if all your child does is run to his room yelling how life is unfair, let it go. Give the child space and time he needs to blow off steam.

When you punish, do not be overly harsh. The way to do this is to refrain from punishing in the heat of your anger. If the child is screaming and yelling at you and you scream back punishments, the situation will only escalate. The child will keep going, and so will you. Here is where many parents lose control. However, if you take a moment, breath and ask yourself, "What lesson do I want my child to take from this?" The answer will give you a perspective on what you should do. It would be a sad affair if you joined your yelling child and yelled too. The secret to avoiding a chaotic home is to control your feelings while teaching your child to do the same.

Teach the Child Constructive Ways to Resolve Problems

Teach the child relaxation techniques like breathing and other self-calming tools that deflate anger and stress. This way, the child will take charge of his emotions even without needing help. These techniques not only work to lower agitation, but they also influence impulse control. The child may not get it or begin to practice immediately, but with encouragement and guidance, they will get better at it. For example, if you teach the child how to breathe in when he gets the urge to punch the wall, succeeding in this will make him gain a sense of control over what he feels and this lessens the possibility of acting out in other ways.

Model Proper Anger Expression

Heard of the expression 'Actions are louder than words'? Yes, children learn better from what the adults are modeling than from what is told to them. Even in your own life, you are likely to read into someone's character from what they do better than what they speak. We tend to exaggerate or give a false report in our speech but the real character comes out in the way we act. Therefore, if you as a parent becomes aggressive when overcome with anger, your child is likely to pick up that trait too. You will be teaching them that it is okay to hit others, yell, and become mean at the slightest provocation.

I bet you would prefer that your child dealt with anger appropriately. You want the child to learn how to regulate emotions, internalize their actions and thoughts, address the anger source, and think about how the child's reaction affects the situation and other people.

Although it is best to shield a child from adult issues, grab an opportunity to demonstrate a healthy way to deal with anger and frustration. It does not only demonstrate appropriate behavior; the kid gets to see that adults can be angry also. For example, if someone in your household leaves a tap running, say "I am angry that this person left the water running, but I will close the tap so that the water bill does not get so big." In saying this, the child will learn how to keep emotions in check and to take action.

In the event you are caught off guard and your child heard you yell or sees you behave irrationally, apologize for it. Tell the child that you are sorry and that you should have done better. Say "I am deeply sorry that you got to hear me yell when I was angry today. I was wrong to react that way. I should have gone to take a walk instead of raising my voice." With this statement, you get to correct your child's perception of the situation. However, do not repeatedly be caught doing the same thing, your apology will achieve the opposite result. The child will learn that it is okay to behave irrationally so long as you can give an apology to cover it all up later.

Avoid Subjecting the Child to Violent Influences

The least influence an angry child needs is which is brought by a violent atmosphere. Some parents believe that their children are unaffected by their angry outbursts, but the truth is children emulate everything they see. They read into the emotional atmosphere in the family to determine how safe they are. If the child perceives that the environment is not accommodating, he develops chronic anxiety or stress and at the slightest provocation, the child will fly off the handle just like his parents do.

Since a child's mind is still being shaped, a violent movie or video game causes them to think aggressive thoughts. You are able to distinguish between fiction and reality in a movie, though this ability slips from us sometime. However, a child will perceive that that's the way the world works. Keep off aggressive video games and movies, and ensure that the child has no access to them also.

Songs promoting violence or becoming friends with bullies also have the same effect because they program a child's mind thereby making him prone to aggression.

Family Member

The techniques you will need to deal with angry family members are similar to those you use to deal with your own anger, your partner's anger, and that of an angry child. If you have already mastered those ones, applying the knowledge to this situation will be easy. The techniques are:

- Control yourself.
- Be patient and respectful.
- Be firm and polite.
- Determine what triggers their anger.
- Show compassion and care.
- Indicate your desire to help them work through their emotions.

Chapter 7: Facts About Anger

Having discussed anger in depth, you already know what anger is, can identify signs of anger, know the origin of anger, its triggers and how to control it and to help others do the same. However, this chapter seeks to provide a more comprehensive and ordered description of facts about anger.

Here are some facts you need to know about anger.

- *Anger is not a bad emotion.*

    The belief that anger is bad is misconceived. In fact, anger is a natural emotion or response to an unsafe or uncharacteristic situation. There is nothing bad or good about a response, it is just a response. It is the driver that makes people confront unfairness and injustice. Just as hunger prompts you to eat, hunger prompts you to take action over an unfair situation.

- *Anger is not aggression.*

    Although anger and aggression are born of the same circumstances, they are quite different. Anger is the emotion or the frustration a person gets when expectations are not met. Aggression is the behavior by negative emotion that causes a person to want to destroy something or hurt someone such as by hitting, shoving, or slapping him/her. Foul language and name-calling are also part of the aggressive behavior. In essence, anger is the emotion that drives aggression.

- *Anger can motivate.*

We have established that anger causes a person to want to respond to an unfair situation or treatment. This response comes because anger causes a surge in energy that causes a person to feel indomitable. Although it is difficult to know what to do at the moment, the residual emotion can drive you to come up with a solution to a problem.

- *It is often a surface emotion.*

If you make an inquiry on what caused someone to act up when angry, you are likely to hear many responses starting with "I do not know what came over me..." This is not to mean that some alien being took control over the person, it means that they were not reacting to the unfair or rude treatment. Anger is more complicated than that. It originates from memories of pain and trauma experienced in the past which causes someone to become quite irritable at the slightest trigger. However, present factors like hunger, extreme thirst, pain, and extreme weather can put you on edge.

- *Anger indicates coping ability.*

Anger causes frustration and irritation that you may not even have to express in aggression. As different aggravating situations come along, you get to see how much of it you can bear. However, in the event you realize that you are not able to cope with a certain level of irritation in your life, you may seek for ways to help overcome that, including going for therapy. The secret to coping, however, is not in suppressing anger, but your ability to channel its energy to other productive ventures.

- *Anger affects your physiology.*

  You may have noted changes in your body physiology when you became angry. Some people's heartbeat increases, muscles tense up, palms sweat while others start feeling their stomachs ache. Anger causes the release of adrenaline in the body, to charge you to either fight or fly. You are advised to express anger because when you do not, it feeds off itself affecting your physiology and the nervous system.

- *Anger causes life-threatening diseases and conditions.*

  Chronic anger eats you off in the form of illnesses. When you are unable to overcome some form of pain and in return, it brings back bouts of anger, you can become physically ill or suffer conditions like heart attack and stroke. An unhealthy diet, smoking, failure to exercise, and other negative coping methods aggravate the effects of anger thereby increasing a person's susceptibility to serious heart conditions and diseases.

- *Anger is predictable.*

  In an unpleasant or unfair situation, you would expect that a person would feel bad and become angry. The person will even be more upset if the unfair situation can be avoided and is only done by choice. This is the reason kids can predict how much their parents can be angry if they do something against the rules. Deception heightens anger levels.
- *Uncontrolled anger initiates problems.*

We associate anger with negative things because we understand that it can cause problems for people. Majority of those serving time in prison acted on anger and hurt others or damaged property. Anger also causes physical fights, arguments, damages relationships, and causes accidents that maim or kill. Some angry people result in substance use and abuse that cause health problems and death in the end. Uncontrolled anger is one of society's most dangerous poisons.

- *A person does not necessarily trigger anger.*

People are not the default sources of anger. The environment too can be a source of frustration and stress. For example, noise pollution for people living near airports, construction zones, train stations, and busy highways can trigger extreme anger even without them knowing. If you feel anger and cannot trace its source, how about listening to your environment to determine what could be annoying to you.

- *Humor beats anger.*

However angry you are, try laughing and voila! You will be on your high spirits again. Ever noticed how a funny comment lets your guard down during an argument? That is the beauty of laughter; it diffuses negative emotions and gets you smiling again. Although your concerns will continue to exist, you will be able to address them when calmer.

- *Relaxation reduces anger.*

Exercise, a good diet, and relaxation are the key antidotes for beating anger. If you are in a happy and relaxed mood, it is likely that a screaming child or a negative comment will just pass you by. You will barely notice it.

- *Blowing off steam is a bad idea.*

While punching a pillow is more socially acceptable than punching a face when angry, it may not do you good in the long run. It is obviously better to spare others from the effects of your anger by withdrawing to cool off, but this can intensify your anger issues. You develop aggression and are not able to exercise the ability to control yourself.

- *Anger is a gender thing.*

Although I would want to keep myself from discussing gender in this issue, it does play a role in how we express anger in society. In the West, and possibly across the globe also, anger is considered a masculine thing. Each gender is taught differently in regards to anger management. Girls are required to be passive while boys are encouraged to be aggressively angry. Adult men are likely to express anger physically by punching something while women find it hard to express it but with tears. As a result, women keep anger longer than men do. However, neither of the sexes has adopted a good coping method.

Chapter 8: Anger Management Goals

Anger management is good for a number of reasons. It helps people identify their stressors, monitor their reaction to it, let out the anger in a positive manner, and identify the origin of this vicious cycle. People are taught how to stay calm in heated environments, how to respond to angry people, and when to walk out of the situation.

However, the ultimate anger management goal is simple. It is to help a person reduce his anger. Anger is reduced when you are able to take charge of the physical and emotional stimulation it causes. It is impossible to avoid all situations and persons that can provoke you to anger but you can learn to respond to these people and situations in a cool manner.

One of the most popular misconceptions is that anger management is meant to give you anger suppression skills, but this is not the case. In fact, preventing anger is not a feasible goal. Anger is a normal emotion and you will experience it regardless of the effort you make to avoid it. Anger management skills and therapy only come in to try to unmask the reason behind the intense negative emotions and to express them in a healthy way. When you manage anger in this manner, you will not only feel lighter, but your past unmet needs, hurts, and pains will be addressed. You become a champion at addressing issues in your life and helping others address issues affecting them.

Learning anger management skills takes time and a lot of self-evaluation work, but the more you do it, the easier it gets. The payoffs also make it worth trying, at least. You build better relationships, repair broken ones, maintain your health, and live a more satisfying life.

Anger Management Therapy

Some people find it rather difficult to get to the core of their anger issues and will need professional help doing that. Others have difficulty practicing relaxation techniques while others are unable to channel the energy they get from anger to a healthy cause. Sometimes you may assume that you finally have a grip of it and your confidence crumbles down on your next outburst. This is where a therapist steps in.

When going through anger management therapy, a client receives guidance and training on a number of recovery guidelines. Clients get to have a platform on which they can release their emotions safely and in a controlled manner. In therapy, the expression is guided by questions. With these questions, the therapist primarily seeks to extract productive responses from the client.

The primary advantage of taking therapy rather than doing the anger management process on your own is that therapy gets deeper to the problems underlying. Clients still get to examine their anger triggers, analyze the emotions they feel in each stage of arousal, and learn to look out for the signs that precede anger. It is also typical of angry people to be in denial, which means that managing anger by themselves may not be as productive as it would be guided by a professional. Therapists are also able to analyze the body's response to past, current, and future events by examining their emotional reaction to specific stimuli. This process is meant to identify the body's defense mechanisms that could impede treatment.

An important thing to take note is that anger management is not only designed to help the victims, but it also helps the people surrounding them. For example, if you have an angry spouse or an angry child, you can take up therapy to learn how to handle them properly. Exposure to uncontrollable anger may lead to serious psychological, physiological, and physical problems for you. However, therapy will help you manage your response to an angry outburst and equip you with skills to help your loved one calm down.

Clients taking anger management therapy have the option of taking their classes individually or in a group setting. Individual therapy involves the client working with the professional one-on-one. It is particularly suitable for clients with privacy issues such as those who may not be comfortable talking about deep sensitive issues to a group of people. Other clients choose it for its convenience to their schedules. Meanwhile, group therapy calls for clients to go through treatment as a team. A class is designed to address a particular issue, which means that persons in each class have experienced the same problem and are able to relate and empathize with each other. Examples of classes include the work-related anger class, teen class, relationship issues class, and the teen class.

The classes are available continually at the treatment centers or as an online course. Therapists give home exercises and assignments because these are thought to make the process more efficient. People in therapy are also encouraged to practice the skills they learn in their day-to-day life. Therapy, therefore, allows the clients to learn and practice concurrently, which improves their understanding and the ability to control anger. In addition, if a technique is not working, the therapist can dig up another based on his experience in the practice.

Professional services are also superior to personal home treatment because anger is often tied to other serious mental health problems. It is likely that a therapist will diagnose these problems in the course of treating anger. These conditions include a narcissistic personality, depression, bipolar disorder, posttraumatic stress disorder (PTSD), and oppositional defiant disorder (ODD). These conditions cause a person to have uncontrollable anger outbursts at the least provocation. Children that are exhibiting extreme hostility and anger could be suffering from ODD. If basic control strategies are not working, it is best to try professional help because it might result in a diagnosis, which is a step towards treatment.

Professional help is also important because chronic anger leads to behavioral problems. People who suffer from constant eruptions of anger are more likely to take on substance abuse, which typically starts at an early age. Teens who abuse drugs rarely complete or further their education. The use of drugs also significantly ruins a user's ability to control their impulses. These people, therefore, need urgent intervention in the form of therapy.

A therapist is devoted to helping her clients acquire skills to manage their overpowering emotions. The services may also help to address underlying pain and memories that could be the root of the distress. With patience and persistence, it is possible to control any anger level.

Persons Who Can Benefit

Our judicial system is at liberty to mandate persons sued for aggression and anger-related issues to attend court-ordered anger management class to help them regain control of their anger. Typically, these people have committed criminal offenses, but offenses like battery and assault, destruction of property, disturbance of the peace, and violence against an intimate partner also get people taking these mandatory classes.

Persons working in the health care and business fields are advised to take anger management classes to avoid the risk of becoming irritated and frustrated while handling customers. People seeking to improve the nature of their relationships with their children, friends, and family members are also suitable candidates for this class. Other social groups to whom this therapy is recommended include persons who use or are recovering from substance use and misuse, those suffering from traumatic brain injury, and persons with mental health problems. Violent criminals and bullies are also advised to seek professional help managing their anger.

Conclusion

Thanks for making it through to the end of *Anger Management: Ultimate Guide to Master Your Emotions, Identify, and Control Anger to Completely Take Back Your Life*, let's hope it was informative and able to provide you with all the tools you need to achieve your goals whatever they may be. Certainly, you were able to refresh your memory and learn new things about anger, detecting it, and resolving it for you and for those around you.

Anger is a healthy emotion that is common to all, but most people lose their temper at some point in their lives. Those who do not have outbursts today did have them at some point in life however blatant or subtle it may be, nevertheless, they learned to control and channel it properly. This should be a ray of hope because it shows that you, your partner, child, or family member can achieve the same through consistent practice.

The next step is to dip your feet right into the pool and begin to practice what you read therein. While you may have already mastered some of the steps indicated, whether pertaining to your anger issue or of those around you, feel free to start the process afresh. Starting the process all over again will not hurt, it will only make you an expert at what you are doing. You might also be lucky enough to notice new things you had not identified before. After all, our bodies and emotions evolve continually.

If you experience difficulty taking up the process of managing anger by yourself, know that it is important to seek professional help. Anger management therapists are trained to help you overcome anger in a controlled way and in a safe space. As discussed earlier, you will find that the therapy sessions are structured strategically to handle your issue in one-on-one sessions or in active interaction with like-minded people in a group session.

Lastly, if you enjoyed this book, I ask that you please take the time to review it on Audible.com. Your honest feedback would be greatly appreciated.

Thank you.

Now, I would like to share with you a free sneak peek to another one of my books that I think you will really enjoy. The book is called "Self Compassion: The Mindful Path to Understand your Emotions" by Kirstin Germer, Christopher Neff and it's A Practical Guide to Learn the Proven Power of Self-Acceptance, Self-Criticism, Self-Awareness and Mindfulness. You will also learn how to be Kind to Yourself and Move On.

Enjoy!

Introduction

Fostering a sense of self-compassion and self-acceptance can be challenging even for a healthy and well-rounded adult. Despite how important these two characteristics are, very few people are taught about how to utilize them in their personal lives. Instead, we are often taught to be hard on ourselves, push ourselves as far as we can, and demand the maximum results out of our efforts. While challenging yourself to achieve substantial growth is valuable, pushing yourself to the point where it becomes self-sabotaging is not a positive habit to support.

If you truly want to achieve all of the success that you desire in life, you need to have a clear understanding of your mental wellbeing and around how you can support it so that you can improve your chances of succeeding. Without a strong mindset to back them up, most people will fail to achieve their desired level of success because despite having the best of intentions, they will struggle to keep themselves focused and motivated. Through the emotional and mental self-sabotaging behaviors such as having an overly harsh inner critic or trying to push through challenging emotions without acknowledging their purpose or healing them, they will simply burn out and fail to thrive.

As you go through this book, realize that you are going to be granted every single tool you need to begin developing the skills to become more self-compassionate and self-accepting. From identifying how to feel your emotions and develop a relationship to building a productive mindfulness and self-awareness practice, everything is devoted to helping you motivate yourself in a healthy way. The tools in this book will not encourage or motivate you to become complacent, lose focus, or stop aiming for your dreams with any less intensity than you already have been. Instead, they will support you in having a stronger focus on how you can achieve your goals without compromising your inner sense of wellbeing. As a result, all of the success that you earn in your life will feel far more meaningful and positive.

If self-compassion has been particularly challenging for you until now, or if the concept itself seems foreign, I encourage you to really set the intention to approach this book and the subjects within it with an open mind. You will get the most out of each chapter and all of the tools provided if you give yourself permission to see things from a new perspective at least for the duration of this book. Fully embrace the practice of not only learning about and understanding these concepts and tools but actually working towards putting them into practice in your life as well. As you begin to see just how powerful they are and how they support you in moving forward towards a more positive future, you will quickly begin to realize why they matter so much.

Lastly, there is one major concept that you need to realize before you begin going through this book. That is — self-compassion is an act of self-care, but it is also a tool that is learned through personal development practices. You are not going to be able to achieve self-compassion all in one attempt, nor will you truly be able to measure or grade yourself on the level of self-compassion that you currently have or that you develop. While there are ways for you to track your improvements and we will go into detail on those ways later, you need to understand that this practice is solely about helping yourself feel better and feel more positive in your approach to life. By allowing yourself to embody that balance, you will begin to feel far more peaceful overall.

Now, if you are ready to embark on the next chapter of your journey in self-development, it is time that you begin! Remember, self-compassion is a powerful tool for you to equip yourself with, so approach this book as open-mindedly as you possibly can. And of course, enjoy the process!

Chapter 1: Understanding the Self

Your Self or your identity is an important element of who you are. When you consider who you are, the illusion that you come up with is how you identify yourself. Although we tend to believe that our selves are an inherent part of who we are and that our personal beliefs over ourselves are finite and final, the reality is that who we are and who we think we are, typically reflect two entirely different people. Many people fail to realize that there is a difference and often find themselves genuinely believing that they are the person whom they envision in their minds and that there is no other alternative or option. As a result, they may end up developing a highly toxic, unrealistic, and self-sabotaging image or belief around who they are.

Realizing that who you truly are and who you think you are is two different people can come as a sense of relief to many. When you discover that there is a good chance that you do not actually align with the images or beliefs you have created, you realize that there is an opportunity for you to see yourself in a new light. You may even get the opportunity to start seeing yourself more clearly for who you really are, rather than for the illusion that you have been holding onto in your mind. In fact, by detaching from the strict identity you have held onto in your mind, you can give yourself the opportunity to begin experiencing far more compassion towards yourself in your life.

Identity is a rather complex topic that extends far beyond the image we carry of ourselves and the image that other's carry. In fact, there is an entire psychological study devoted to understanding identity and your sense of self and helping you discover exactly "who" you are. This field of study is known as social science and is comprised of psychologists and researchers who are actively seeking to understand identity to an even deeper level and get a clear sense of what makes a person's identity. Because there are so many different levels of identity, the study itself is quite expansive and continues to discover what one's true identity is versus the way they identify themselves and the way others identify them. In the following sections, you are going to get a deeper insight into what your sense of self truly is, how it is made up, and how your sense of self impacts the way you live your life.

Discovering the Multiple Selves

There are two ways that people have multiple sense of self. The first way that you can experience multiple senses of self comes from how you interact with the people around you and the identity you possess around these people. For example, the self you are around your friends is likely quite different from the self you are around your family or your co-workers. Your environment is a huge factor in which role you will play, depending on where you are and who you are actively surrounded by. The second way that you experience multiple social selves is determined between the way you perceive yourself and the way others perceive you. Since everyone has had their own unique interactions and experiences with you, it is not unreasonable to realize that everyone sees you slightly different from how others see you. For example, your best friend may see you completely different from how your other friends may see you, or your Grandma may carry a completely different belief of who you are compared to the rest of the world. The relationship that people share with you, the experiences that you share together, and their perception of you and of people in general will all impact how people identify you. As a result, you actually have multiple identities – and no, that does not mean that you are having an identity crisis or that you have something wrong with you. It is actually entirely normal to have many identities.

When it comes to identifying yourself, you must realize that on a psychological front, you are not identifying yourself as one person inhabiting one body. You are identifying yourself based on the actual identity that you carry or the characteristics and personality traits that you are perceived to have. Your "self" is the conscious aspect of you that interacts with the world around you, communicates with other people, and shares experiences with others. Although there is no scientific evidence that proves that there is an out-of-body "self," most psychologists believe that the self is not attached to or identified by a person's body. Instead, it is the dimension of you that exists in your mind or the aspects of you that make up "who" you are beyond your physical and biological self.

This part of yourself that is not defined by your body or biology is typically described in three related but separable domains when it comes to psychological understanding. This means that there are three elements that coincide to make up your "self" or your identity. The first domain is known as your experiential self which is also known as the 'theatre of consciousness.' This part of yourself is identified as your first-person sense of being or how you personally experience the world around you. This part of yourself remains consistent over periods of time which results in psychologists believing that it is very closely linked to your memory. The second part of your identity is what is known as your private self-consciousness. This is your inner narrator or the voice that verbally narrates what is happening in your life to you privately within your mind. When you are reading, learning, or interpreting the world around you, this voice is actively narrating how you are interpreting that information and what sense you are making of it. This is the part of you that carries your beliefs and values about how the world works. Neuroscientist Antonio Damasio calls your private self-consciousness your autobiographical self because it is regularly narrating your autobiography in your mind. The third and final dimension of your identity is your public self or your persona. This is the image that you attempt to project to others through your actions, attitudes, behaviors, and words. This is the part of your self that other people interact with and see which results in this being the part of yourself that people generate perceptions around. It is through your persona that people determine what your identity is according to them and their own understanding.

With all that being said, the multiple selves that you embody comes from the persona that you share with others. People will then generate perceptions around who you are, what your identity is, and how they feel about that. It is through this persona that people will decide if they can relate to you, if they like you, and anything else relating to how they feel about you. In realizing that people generate their perceptions of you based off of one single aspect of who you truly are, it helps you realize that their perspective is not accurate. In fact, neither is yours. No one, including yourself, *truly* knows who you actually are. Everything is just generated based on beliefs, values, perspectives, and understandings that have been accumulated through varying life experiences.

Relationship with Ourselves

The relationship that you share with yourself often develops somewhere between the first and second dimensions of your identity. The way you interpret and interact with the world around you, combined with your beliefs and values helps you generate a sort of self-awareness that allows you to begin determining what you believe your identity is. Again, just like with other people, your identity is largely based off of your perception and understanding of the world around you and how it works. Even if your own perception is rarely accurate when compared to who you actually are which is a unique blend of all three layers of your dimensional identity.

Because your relationship with yourself is largely defined by your beliefs and values and your ability to live in alignment with them or not, it is easy to realize that how you identify yourself can be easily shifted based on your perceptions. If you carry certain core beliefs about how people should live, for example, and you are not living in alignment with those beliefs, then you may generate a perception that identifies you as someone who is bad or unworthy. You might relate yourself to the identities you have mentally designed for other people in society who you believe to be bad too which can result in you seeing yourself in an extremely negative light. If you carry certain core beliefs about how people should live and you *are* living in alignment with them, you may praise yourself and see yourself as good and special. You might then find yourself relating more to people in society who you see as good and positive, thus allowing you to cast yourself in a positive light.

The reality is that none of us are truly inherently good or bad, we are all just perceiving, experiencing, and responding to the world around us. Generating internal images of what is positive and what is not only results in you setting standards for yourself on how you should behave. If these standards are beyond what you can reasonably achieve or do not align with what you genuinely want in life, then you may find yourself adhering to beliefs and values that are actually rather destructive. Instead of helping you live a life of contentment and satisfaction, you may find these beliefs leading to you constantly feeling incapable and under confident. As a result, your relationship with yourself may deteriorate because the way in which you view yourself is not reasonable or compassionate.

Everyone Has Their Own Filters and Explanatory Styles

To help you develop your understanding of how your perception of yourself varies from other's perception of you, let's discuss personal filters and explanatory styles. Understanding why everyone has such different views of the world allows you to have a stronger understanding as to why there are so many aspects of your identity based on your own personas and the way that people perceive them and you. The concept of personal filters and explanatory styles is simple. A personal filter is how you see the world and your explanatory style is how you explain it to yourself and to others.

Every single person has a unique filter and explanatory style that is based on their own unique experiences in life. All of the interactions they have had, the situations they have encountered, and things they have been told by the people around them shape the way that they view life itself. How each of these small yet impactful things come together will shape how each person perceives the world around them, others that cohabit the planet with them, and themselves. So, for example, if someone along the way has learned that not washing your dishes every day is a sign of laziness and ignorance, then that person is going to believe that anyone who leaves dishes in the sink overnight is somehow "bad," including themselves.

The foundation of a person's filters and explanatory styles are rooted in childhood when a child is not yet able to generate their own independent thoughts and beliefs. Until we are six years old, our ability to critically think about things and generate our own opinions independent of the opinions of others is virtually non-existent so we absorb everything we learn. This means that anything your parents said, people around you were saying, or you were shown through other's behaviors and actions were anchored into your mind as the foundation of your personal beliefs and values. Even though you gained the capacity to think critically and start generating your own opinions around six years old, you were still actively internalizing what everyone told you because, in most cases, no one ever taught you otherwise. As a result, you likely have many different beliefs and values that stemmed in your childhood which have gone on to impact you for years to come. In fact, these very beliefs and values are believed to make up a lot of what your autobiographical-self narrates to yourself on a daily basis, thus shaping the way you see yourself. See, who you think you are may not even be an accurate reflection of how *you* think, it may actually be an internalization based on the beliefs and values you were taught by people as you were growing up.

Since every single person will hear different things throughout their lives even if they are raised in similar environments, the way that every person views and interprets the world around them varies. Even siblings will grow up to have different perceptions and beliefs based on the way that they have internalized the beliefs they heard and were shown throughout their lifetimes. It is through this process that each person develops their own personal filters and explanatory styles for how they interpret and explain the world around them. Because of this, we can conclude that any beliefs that you have around who you are and any beliefs that others have around who you are do not actually define who you truly are. Instead, they define the belief systems that you have established throughout your life until this point.

When you realize that your beliefs are what shape your *perception* of your identity and not your identity itself, it becomes a lot easier for you to have compassion for yourself.

You begin to realize that how you see yourself is not necessarily a true reflection of who you are, but instead a way that you have been lead to view yourself. This view was designed to support you in feeling connected to your 'tribe' or family and community, but in some cases, it can become destructive and result in you feeling deeply disconnected from yourself. When that happens, realizing that you are not inherently 'bad' or 'wrong' because you do not feel like you fit in makes it a lot easier for you to have compassion for your feelings and for the experiences you are going through. As a result, healing from these painful emotions and moving forward into a more self-compassionate and self-loving future becomes a lot easier for you.

Thank your, this preview is now over.

If you enjoyed this preview of my book "The Mindful Path to Self-Compassion" by Frank Steven, be sure to check out the full book on amazon.com

Thank you.

POSITIVE THINKING:
POWERFUL DAILY AFFIRMATIONS TO TRAIN YOUR BODY AND MIND

Program Your Brain Against Negative Thoughts to Attract Success and Abundance

TABLE OF CONTENTS

- INTRODUCTION 119
- SUCCESS AFFIRMATION 120
- SUCCESS AFFIRMATIONS 134
- POSITIVE AFFIRMATIONS 135
- LOVE LIFE AFFIRMATION 156
- ABUNDANCE AFFIRMATION 172
- HEALTHY BRAIN AFFIRMATION 189
- HAPPINESS AFFIRMATION 204
  - TO START YOUR DAY WITH A STRONG AND HEALTHY RELATIONSHIP: 229
  - TO START YOUR DAY WITH ABUNDANCE AND SUCCESS: 230
  - TO START YOUR DAY WITH HOPE, CONFIDENCE, AND FEELING POSITIVE: 231
  - TO START YOUR DAY FREE OF WORRY, STRESS, AND NEGATIVE FEELINGS: 232
  - TO START YOUR DAY WITH GREATNESS AND MOTIVATION: 233
  - TO START YOUR DAY FOCUSING ON YOUR WORK AND CAREER: 233
- CONCLUSION 235
- STAY FIT AFFIRMATIONS 236

Introduction

Congratulations on purchasing Positive Thinking: Be Happy and Love Life with Powerful Affirmations, and thank you for doing so!

The following chapters will provide you with Affirmations to condition Your Body and Mind to Natural Happiness Every Day. It will help you to Program Your Brain to become Healthy, Attract Success and Abundance.

Thanks again for choosing this audiobook! Every effort was made to ensure it is full of as much useful information as possible. Please enjoy!

Success Affirmation

I have the power to create all the success and prosperity I desire.

I let go of old, negative beliefs that have stood in the way of my success.

My mind is free of resistance and open to exciting new possibilities.

I am worthy of all the good life has to offer, and I deserve to be successful.

I believe in myself and my ability to succeed.

I am grateful for all my skills and talents that serve me so well.

I am enjoying my work today and optimistic about the coming days.

The universe is filled with endless opportunities for me and my career.

I am surrounded by positive, supportive people who believe in me.

I am always open minded and eager to explore new avenues to success.

Whatever I can dream up for my business, I can achieve.

I attract my ideal clients and customers with my energy. My ideal clients come to me easily.

I love every experience, client and prospect I've ever had.

My brand gives more value than it takes in financial gain.

My Business helps thousands and thousands of people. My brand solves real problems for real people.

My brand is always leaving people in a more positive state then when they began.

I have an authentic brand that creates and rallies people around a positive cause.

My brand is a leader in the industry. It paves the way for others to create and understand their reality.

My brand represents a set of positive values that I live my life by.

I am in business to help people, and to positively change the world.

I have an extremely engaged tribe and community that supports me.

My brand changes people, for the better.

I am passionate. I am outrageously enthusiastic and inspire others.

I allow my brand to be more than I've ever dreamed of. I am known for my positive energy and abundant lifestyle.

My positive attitude, confidence and hard work naturally draws in new opportunities.

I am enthusiastic and excited about my work.

My enthusiasm about my job is contagious.

My workplace is peaceful and full of love.

I make decisions easily.

I speak positively about my coworkers and they respond by speaking positively about me.

I am rewarded for doing my best.

I engage in healthy stimulation during my breaks.

I eat healthy, nutritious food during my lunch break and my body is grateful, granting me energy and good health in return.

I am an excellent employee, always productive and giving my best effort.

I am experiencing success in my career.

I enjoy working toward future career success.

I have a satisfying job.

I know exactly what I need to do to achieve success in my career.

My work environment is calm and productive.

The job I have is perfect for me.

I am experiencing wealth every day.

I am financially successful in all my endeavors.

I am getting wealthier each day.

I am living the life of my dreams.

I have enough wealth to fulfill my desires

I radiate success

I was born to be successful, it is my natural state of being.

The power is within me. I learn from the past, live in the now and plan for the future.

I am in control of my emotions, desires and abilities.

I trust in my capacity for greatness. I believe I am worthy of great success.

I live a beautiful life and I only attract the best of everything.

I am at peace with where I am and I have a strong vision for my future.

I am breaking through old, limiting patterns of behaviour and becoming more successful every day.

I love that opportunities to be successful are all around me, every day.

I celebrate the success I have in my life in every moment.

I am rich in love, wealth and happiness.

I recognize opportunity when it knocks and seize the moment.

Every day I discover interesting and exciting new paths to pursue.

When I need help, I effortlessly attract the perfect resources and solutions.

Everywhere I look, I see prosperity.

I am well organized and manage my time with expert efficiency.

I am committed to achieving success in every area of my life.

I love my job, and my work is a fulfilling part of my journey to greater success.

My ambitions are in perfect alignment with my personal values.

I work with fascinating, inspiring people who all share my enthusiasm.

By creating success for myself I am creating success and opportunities for others.

As I take on new challenges I feel calm, confident, and powerful.

Creating solutions comes naturally to me.

I always attract successful people who understand and encourage me.

I recognize every new challenge as a new opportunity.

I celebrate each goal I accomplish with joy and gratitude.

The more successful I become, the more confident I feel.

I consistently attract just the right circumstances at just the right time.

I am grateful for all the abundance flowing into my life.

I trust my intuition and am always guided to make wise decisions.

I stay focused on my vision and pursue my daily work with passion.

Every day is filled with new ideas that inspire and motivate me.

I excel in all that I do, and success comes easily to me.

I always expect a positive outcome and I naturally attract good results.

I take pride in my ability to make worthwhile contributions to the world.

I attract brilliant mentors who graciously share their wisdom and guidance.

I step outside my comfort zone with courage and confidence.

I am a patient listener and an effective communicator.

As I allow more abundance into my life, more doors open for me.

I am free of stress and I thrive under pressure.

I set high standards for myself and always live up to my expectations.

I have an endless supply of new ideas that help me become more and more successful.

I have released all limiting beliefs about my ability to succeed.

Every day I dress for success in body, mind, and spirit.

I think big and dream big without reservation.

I love who I am and I naturally attract people who respect me as a unique individual.

I am creating a life of abundance and happiness.

I am successfully living up to my full potential.

I am making the world a better place by being a positive, powerful influence.

I am grateful for my financial success.

I am living the dream!

My body is healthy; my mind is brilliant; my soul is tranquil.

I believe I can do anything.

Everything that is happening now is happening for my ultimate good.

I am the architect of my life; I built its foundation and choose its contents.

I forgive those who have harmed me in my past and peacefully detach from them.

My ability to conquer my challenges is limitless; my potential to succeed is infinite.

Today, I abandon my old habits and take up new positive ones.

I can achieve greatness.

Today, I am brimming with energy and overflowing with joy.

I love and accept myself for who I am.

Life supports me in every possible way.

I am in the process of making positive changes in all areas of my life.

It does not matter what other people say or do. What matters is how I choose to react and what I choose to believe about myself.

I am good enough.

I forgive everyone in my past for all the perceived wrongs. I release them with love.

I let go of all fear and doubt, and life becomes simple and easy for me.

Everything I need comes to me at the perfect time.

I feel glorious, dynamic energy. I am active and alive.

Today is going to be a really, really good day.

I am beautiful and everybody loves me.

I deserve only good in my life.

My good is constantly coming to me, so I relax and enjoy my life.

I can do it.

I deserve the best and I accept the best now."

I release all resistance to attracting money. I am worthy of a positive cash flow."

I practice forgiveness daily so that I cam free to move beyond the past into the present moment."

I love and appreciate myself."

"I act as if I already have what I want, it's an excellent way to attract happiness in my life."

"I am willing to change and grow."

I love every cell of my body."

I awaken today, appreciating everything in sight, and I give thanks.

I rejoice in the love I encounter every day."

All that I need to know at any given moment is revealed to me.

My intuition is always on my side.

I now free myself from destructive fears and doubts."

I am a unique and beautiful soul."

I am grateful for every experience I have ever had as it has shaped me into the person I am today, and that is exactly who I am supposed to be right this very moment."

I enjoy today and cheerfully look forward to tomorrow.

I choose to make the rest of my life the best of my life."

"I give my body what it needs.

I trust the process of life to always be here for me."

Today I mentally wrap each person I meet in a circle of love."

Abundance flows freely through me."

I am surrounded by love. All is well."

Life brings me only good experiences. I am open to new and wonderful changes."

I trust myself."

My mental pattern is positive and joyful."

I am a magnet for money. Prosperity of every kind is drawn to me."

Every moment presents a wonderful new opportunity to become more of who I am."

I lovingly do everything I can to assist my body in maintaining perfect health."

I am deeply fulfilled by all that I do."

I have plenty of time to do what I need to do.

Time expands for me."

I am an open channel for creative ideas.

I give myself permission to be prosperous."

I now see opportunities for abundance everywhere. I am blessed."

My day begins and ends with gratitude and joy."

I affirm that I have the power to heal myself."

Today I look at all the positive things in my life, and I am grateful for them."

"I have the knowledge to make smart decisions for myself."

I have all that I need to make today a great day."

I am, and always will be, enough."

"I acknowledge my own self-worth – my confidence is rising."

I let go of any negative feelings about myself or my life, and accept all that is good."

I always attract only the best of circumstances and I have the best positive people in my life."

I am courageous. I am willing to act and face my fears."

I have unlimited power."

I am a powerful creator. I create the life I want and enjoy it."

Every day I discover interesting and exciting new paths to pursue."

I trust my intuition and I always make wise decisions."

I am focused on my goals and feel passionate about my work."

I work well under pressure and always feel motivated."

I am living to my full potential."

I have everything I need to face any obstacles that come".

I have the power to create all the success and prosperity I desire."

I can let go of old, negative beliefs that have stood in the way of my success"

The universe is filled with endless opportunities for my career."

I am surrounded by supportive, positive people who believe in me and want to see my succeed"

I will be open-minded and always eager to explore new avenues to success."

As I take on new challenges I feel calm, confident, and powerful."

I will celebrate each goal I accomplish with gratitude and joy."

I choose to think positively and create a wonderful and successful life for myself."

I am grateful that my life is so happy and successful."

I can never fail, for everything that happens contributes to me being better."

I am extremely passionate about constantly being better and more successful."

I have the courage to create positive change in my life."

I acknowledge my own self-worth; my self-confidence is rising."

Others look up to me as a leader because of my confidence"

Every day I will become more confident, powerful, and successful"

Feeling confident, assured, and strong is a normal part of my everyday life"

I am self-reliant, creative and persistent in whatever I do."

I am valuable and will make powerful contributions to the world today."

I made decisions based on the superstar I am becoming."

I continuously push myself to learn and develop in areas of life that bring me happiness, freedom, and purpose."

I wake up every morning ready for a new day of exciting possibilities"

I am happy and free because I am me."

I am a strong individual who attracts success and happiness."

My life is a blast of growing opportunity because I never stop creating"

I am energetic and enthusiastic. Confidence is my second nature."

I teach others to believe in me by believing in myself."

My actions are intentional and they bring me closer to my goals."

I am learning to trust the journey."

My mind is clear of self-doubt, and I am ready to embrace every challenge that comes my way."

I am surrounded with people who push me to be my best self."

I have great ideas and make great contributions."

Every challenge I face is an opportunity to grow and improve."

I am the architect of my life; I build its foundation and choose its contents."

My ability to conquer my challenges is limitless; my potential to succeed is infinite."

Today, I abandon my old habits and take up new, more positive ones."

Enter the "now"

Be positive

Be concise

Include action

Include a feeling word

Today, and every day, I choose to be confident

I radiate confidence, certainty and optimism

I courageously open and move through every door of opportunity

I am in charge of my life

I have the power to live my dreams

My mind has unlimited power

I stand up for what I belief in

I act with courage and confidence

I believe in myself

I am creative and think outside the box

I attract success and prosperity with all of my ideas

I wake up and make a difference in this world

My business is growing every single day

I am building something that is greater than myself

I am fulfilling my purpose in life

I am rich in health, wealth and love

Opportunities and advantages come with each door that I open

The more I give to the world, the more I get

What I currently do is serving me towards my higher purpose

I have the power to change my thoughts in a second

I'm allowed to do what I want with my life

I have the power to change myself

I allow myself to play and enjoy life

I am making a difference in this world

I am at peace with all that has happened, is happening, and will happen

I have the power to say yes and say no

I choose to do what matters most to me everyday

Success Affirmations

Today, and every day, I choose to be successful

I make choices based on inspiration and not desperation

I am a magnet for success and good fortune

Today, I am stronger and wiser than I was yesterday

I am a genius and I apply my wisdom everyday

I am a magnet for other likeminded and successful people

Every day, in every way, I am becoming more successful

Prosperity and success is my natural state of mind

I am an example of success and triumph

I demonstrate excellence in everything I do

My life is an adventure filled with opportunity and reward

I am committed to my goals

I bring solutions

Today, and every day, I am moving a step closer to my goals

I am focused on and moving towards my higher purpose

I do meaningful work that positively impacts this world

I am open to opportunities

I am the definition of success

I deserve to be successful

POSITIVE AFFIRMATIONS

I am celebrating feeling light and alive at my perfect body weight of one thirty-five.

I am enjoying the thrill of flying.

I am attracting joy into my life.

I am confidently expressing myself openly and honestly.

I am feeling exhilarated, agile and alive.

I am effectively communicating my needs and desires to my loving partner.

I am looking around me at the faces of the people I am helping and I am thrilled to know that I have made a difference in their life.

I am feeling relaxed and grateful to be sitting here in Hawaii with my toes buried in the warm sand, feeling the warmth of the sun on my face.

I am celebrating feeling light and alive at my perfect body weight of one thirty-five.

I am enjoying the thrill of flying.

I am attracting joy into my life.

I am confidently expressing myself openly and honestly.

I am feeling exhilarated, agile and alive.

I am effectively communicating my needs and desires to my loving partner.

I am looking around me at the faces of the people I am helping and I am thrilled to know that I have made a difference in their life.

I am feeling relaxed and grateful to be sitting here in Hawaii with my toes buried in the warm sand, feeling the warmth of the sun on my face.

I am successful in whatever I do

I plan my work and work my plan

I focus on what is truly essential

I will make the most of new opportunities

Good flows to me, good flows from me

I feel wonderful and alive

I feel the joy of abundance

I speak with confidence and calm assurance

The universe provides for my every want and need

I am healthy and happy

I have a lot of energy

I radiate happiness

I am successful in whatever I do

Everything is getting better every day

My mind is calm

I am always on the path of success & victory

I am peace with myself

I find peace and joy in all aspects of my life

I have value and I matter

I am a success in all that I do

I am happy

I feel joy, love, and abundance

I am one with my inner child

I am amazing

I can do anything

I am prepared to succeed

Positivity is a choice

I am fabulous, funny, and giving

I am outstanding

I am unique and special and most importantly I am me

I am financially free

I am perfect exactly as I am

I focus on what is truly essential

I make positive healthy choices

I am in control of my reactions

I find all solutions within me

All is well in my life

I will make the most of new opportunities

I organize my priorities with clarity

I forgive myself

I am forgiven

I will always be there for myself

I enjoy the variety of life

I am my own guru

I take good care of myself

I am patient with myself

I let go of my past

I am evolving eternally

I know I can always upgrade

There is a gift for me in everything that I experience

I follow my inner guidance

I appreciate my physical body

I treat my body well

I take it easy

I make room for fun and playfulness

I appreciate intimacy

I am very good at letting go

I am grateful for my life

I love being myself

Time is on my side

I surrender to love

I invite bliss

I learn from my past

I am good at walking the talk

I enjoy being taken good care of by the universe

I create my reality on a continuous basis

My body is healthy

I am superior to negative thoughts and low actions

I forgive those who have harmed me in my past and peacefully detach from them

I possess the qualities needed to be extremely successful

My business is growing, expanding, and thriving

My ability to conquer my challenges is limitless

My potential to succeed is infinite

I am courageous and I stand up for myself

My thoughts are filled with positivity and my life is plentiful with prosperity

I am blessed with an incredible family and wonderful friends

I am a powerhouse

My future is an ideal projection of what I envision now

I radiate beauty, charm, and grace

I am conquering my illness

I wake up today with strength in my heart and clarity in my mind

My fears of tomorrow are simply melting away

My life is just beginning

The assertion that something exists or is true

I always have everything I need to be happy

I live a positive life and only attract the best in my life

I am peacefully allowing my life to unfold

Today, and every day, I choose to be happy

I am fun energetic and people love me for it

My life overflows with happiness and love

Today is rich with opportunity and I open my heart to receive them

I take the time to show my friends that I care about them

I am thankful that I get to live another day

I see the world with beauty and color

I deserve whatever good comes my way today

I believe in myself

I radiate confidence, certainty and optimism

I courageously open and move through every door of opportunity

I am in charge of my life

I have the power to love my dreams

My mind has unlimited power

I stand up for what I believe in

I act with courage and confidence

I love myself more everyday

I am blessed with an incredible family and wonderful friends

I always turn in my work complete and on time.

I comprehend what I read quickly.

I enjoy participating in extracurricular activities.

I love learning new things and using them in my life.

I love my classes and my teachers.

I make excellent grades on quizzes and tests.

I study comprehensively for my classes.

Every day I become more successful.

I am successful in my daily life.

I feel powerful and full of energy, capable and confident.

I know my success is real.

I learn from my mistakes and they become stepping stones to my success.

I love challenges, easily find solutions to problems, and move past roadblocks quickly.

I am confident.

I am charismatic.

I am funny.

I am charming.

I trust myself.

I am worthy of attention.

I am worthy of being desired.

I am always in the right place at the right time.

I say exactly the right thing to exactly the right person.

I love myself and approve of myself.

I am a unique person worthy of respect.

I have all the right solutions to all of life's events.

I release the need to prove myself to anyone as I am my own self and I love it that way.

I know that I can create miracles in my life.

As I change my thoughts the world around me changes.

I am proud of myself.

I am receiving the best that life has to offer now.

I am excited about the person I am becoming.

My deepest desires are being fulfilled now.

I am loved and accepted exactly as I am, right here and right now.

I love myself exactly as I am. I no longer wait to be perfect in order to love myself.

As I forgive myself, it becomes easier to forgive others.

I am flexible. I adapt to change quickly.

My mind is filled only with loving, healthy, positive and prosperous thoughts, which ultimately are converted into my life experiences.

I am worthy of a happy life.

I deserve to enjoy this day.

My past is not a reflection of my future.

My future will not cloud my present.

I will succeed today.

I trust my intuition and knowledge.

I am not alone in this world.

I am wise enough to make my own decisions.

I will better today by helping others. Happiness is my patrimony. I embody happiness as my state of being.

I am allowed to take up space.

Every morning I wake up feeling eager to start my day on an upbeat note.

The simple things in life are what bring me the most joy.

Positive vibrations radiate from my thoughts.

Success is my natural state. I will flourish in all of my endeavors.

My happiness will rub off on others and inspire them to feel happy as well.

My inner-peace cannot and will not be tarnished by an outside source

I forgive myself for the mistakes I've made.

I love change and am able to adjust myself to new situations.

My self-esteem is improving every single day.

I am powerful and resilient.

The only way I can ever fail is if I give up. In which, I will never give up.

I choose to surround myself with peaceful, uplifting people.

Nothing is impossible.

I trust myself to make the right choices for me.

I am attentive to my surroundings.

Love exists in the world and within my heart.

Human nature is a beautiful thing.

I am a problem solver. I focus on solutions and always find the best solution.

I always try to see the good in people, even when it gets tough.

I trust my intuition and my inner wisdom is my guide.

I am worthy of everything life has to offer.

I am able to observe my emotions without becoming attached to them.

I am able to remain calm and centered in turbulent situations.

I find relief in the fact that I can always leave any situation.

I take the time to show my friends that I care about them.

I view my body as a temple and I treat it with kindness.

I choose peace.

I surround myself with people who accept me and support me.

My family is a blessing to me.

I let go of worries that deplete my energy.

My thoughts are my reality.

I believe in my ability to change the world with the work that I do.

I am able to channel my anger in a positive manner that isn't destructive.

I substitute my anger for compassion and understanding.

I am full of energy and life.

I am unique and that makes me, me.

My outer self is connected to my inner well-being.

I use fear as encouragement to accomplish all of my goals.

No dream is too big for me to achieve.

I choose to not criticize myself or others around me.

I am healthy.

I am calm.

I am grounded.

I'm able to communicate my needs to people in my life.

I nourish my personal relationships.

I know my wisdom guides me to the right decision.

I may not understand the good in this situation but I know it is there.

I am deeply fulfilled with who I am.

The world around me is full of beauty.

The world around me is full of potential.

I am a useful and productive participant in this world.

I am alive and my body is capable.

I am in control of the way I react to any situation.

I am in tune with my emotions.

No one can dim my inner light.

I have many talents to use and be proud of.

I feel powerful and energized.

I recognize the good in others and the good in me.

I accept and love myself for all that I am.

Ican feel amazing, just by deciding to.

I don't need a reason to feel good.

Knowing is not enough; we must apply. Willing is not enough; we must do.

This too shall pass.

Use me, Lord.

In order to earn more, I must learn more.

I control how I feel.

I always focus on and find the good in everything.

Life doesn't happen to me, it happens for me.

Everything happens for a reason and a purpose, and it serves me.

Strength doesn't come from physical capacity, it comes from an abdominal will.

At any moment I need to be willing to sacrifice what I am, for who I could become.

I would rather have a mind opened by wonder than one closed by belief.

I know that I am of good health.

My business is an all-consuming love affair and I attract whatever I need through it.

I am prosperous, healthy, and happy and I live in abundance.

I open myself to the beauty, joy, and harmony of the Universe and I enjoy it.

I love and respect myself at all times.

There are no failures. I learn from everything I do.

I believe that everything is for my highest good and greatest joy.

I move beyond forgiveness, to understanding, and I have compassion and kindness for myself and others.

I open my heart to love and I radiate love.

I forgive those who need forgiving, for not being what I wanted them to be.

I deserve love and I get it in abundance.

I will speak easily and truthfully to myself and others.

I am a good listener.

I am a good communicator.

I am calm.

I love and trust my creative gifts.

I accept that I am an unlimited being and that I can create anything I want.

I am open to new ideas, people, and situations which will enhance my joy and happiness.

The more love I give the more there is to receive.

I am open to the goodness and abundance of the Universe.

Every day and in every way I am getting better and better

I am abundantly joyful and happy

I am so grateful for my life

I find beauty and joy in ordinary things

My life is a joy. I relax easily and open myself up to delightful surprises

My life is a joy filled with love, fun and friendship

I choose love, joy and freedom, open my heart and allow wonderful things to flow into my life.

Im free , and always have been

I remember myself as the master that I am, the master I have always been.

I know I have mastery over my life by how still I can keep my mind and how alert I am in the now.

I am clear, untouched, and unharmed by all that I have experienced in my life.

I use my power lovingly when I have influence over others

I remember myself as the master that I am, the master I have always been.

I know I have mastery over my life by how still I can keep my mind and how alert I am in the now.

I am clear, untouched, and unharmed by all that I have experienced in my life.

I use my power lovingly when I have influence over others

I am as God created me.

As I become more and more aware of myself as eternal consciousness, I become more peaceful and at ease with all that happens in my life.

Physical reality reflects this peace back to me.

Everything in my life is exactly should be

My relationships are loving and harmonious

am at peace. I trust in the process of life

I am connected to divine love and wisdom.

I am harmonious and at peace regardless of my surroundings

My life is blossoming in perfection

I use my emotions, thoughts and challenges to lead me to deeper, more interesting places within myself.

I am grateful for all that I am

I feel God's love within me - and all around me

I am a channel for loving peaceful energy

I radiate with loving kindness and life mirrors that back to me

Pay attention to your thinking

Focus on what you want -- NOT what you don't want

Use the Power of Metaphor to help you – not hurt you!

Take charge of your brain and mind

Have a sense of humor – because your brain does not.

There is no one better to be than myself

I am enough

I got better every single day

I am an amazing person

All of my problems have solutions

Today I am a leader

I forgive myself for my mistakes

My challenges help me grow

I am perfect just the way I am

My mistakes help me learn and grow

Today is going to be a great day

I have courage and confidence

I can control my own happiness

I have people who love and respect me

I stand up I for what I believe in

I believe in my goals and dreams

Its okay not to know everything

Today I choose to think positive

I can get through everything

I can do everything I put my mind to

I give myself permission to make chances

I can do better next time

I have everything I need right now.

I am capable of so much

Everything will be okay

I am free to make my own choices

I deserve to be love

I can make a difference

Today I choose to be confident

I am in charge of my life

I have the power to make my dreams come true

I believe in myself and my abilities

Good things are going to come to me

I matter

My confidence grow when I step out of my comfort zone

My positive thought creates positive feelings

Today I will weak through my fears

I am open and ready to learn

Everyday is a fresh start

If I fall I will get back again

I am whole

I only compare myself to my self

I can do anything

It is enough to do my best

I can be anything I want to be

I accept who I am

Today is going be an awesome day

I approve of myself and love myself deeply and completely.

Life is happening in this moment.

I trust myself and know my inner wisdom is my best guide.

I have integrity. I am totally reliable. I do what I say.

I act from a place of personal security.

I fully accept myself and know that I am worthy of great things in life.

I choose to be proud of myself.

I accept and embrace all experiences, even unpleasant ones.

I fill my mind with positive and nourishing thoughts.

My confidence, self-esteem, and inner wisdom are increasing with each day.

My immune system is very strong and can deal with any kind of bacteria, germs, and viruses.

Every day my joyous experiences expand.

My appreciation of nature fills me with joy.

The gratitude I feel for my blessings fill my heart with continuous joy.

I allow joy to be part of my core foundation.

My joy radiates outwardly to those I meet.

My joy is contagious; the people I meet are affected positively by its energy.

Joyful moments are a priority in my life.

The sound of children at play fills me with joy.

I seek peace, joy and happiness, and wish the same for everyone.

I am open to experiencing more joyous moments each day.

I now accept my joy comes from within.

Loving and accepting who I am today activates my feel good feelings.

I allow myself to feel joy and appreciation for the people who love and nurture me.

I give myself permission to tap into my joy.

My joyfulness is a natural state of mind.

My joyful experiences are magnets for more of the same.

My creative mind finds reasons to be joyful in everything I do.

My thoughts, words and action support my joyful living.

My service to others brings me joy.

My intention is to foster peace and joy.

Every fiber of my being radiates happiness and joy.

My laughter nurtures my joy.

My joy empowers me to reach for new heights.

I give thanks for all that I have and for all that's yet to come.

I give myself permission to be happy with my achievements.

My joy uplifts, empowers and motivates me.

My happy thoughts attract more joyous experiences.

Those who love me bring me joy.

The simple things in life bring me limitless joy.

Positive memories put a smile on my face and keep joy in my daily life.

I give myself permission to embrace joy and happiness.

I willingly remove the blinders that keep me from seeing my bounty of joy.

Living my fullest potential skyrocket my joy and happiness.

I have learned that going with the flow is the way to go for more joyful moments.

I am filled with joy as I create my vision.

I greet each day with joy and gratitude.

Being joyful and happy is my natural state of mind.

I now choose to relax and be in the moment for more joyful experiences.

As I relax I see the beauty in my surroundings and the positive in my experiences.

I make decisions and choices that support and nurture me.

My business and personal life are aligned for joyous fulfillment.

LOVE LIFE AFFIRMATION

My heart is always open. I am kind to every person I meet.

I am surrounded by love. I attract kind people.

I love unconditionally and without hesitation.

I deserve love. I am loved and appreciated by those around me.

Everywhere I go, I am accompanied by love.

I choose love as my response to others.

I think loving thoughts about everyone.

I feel divine love in my heart.

I make choices that are deeply loving.

The love in my heart expands and grows daily.

My intentions are always loving and kind.

I feel deep love in my core.

I live in an ocean of divine love.

My love is unconditional.

I am an expression of divine love.

I love the divine spirit within me.

I admire and respect my partner.

I communicate openly with my spouse and resolve conflicts with respect.

I enjoy the time I spend with my spouse and we have fun together.

I have loving relationship with my spouse.

I love my partner exactly as they are, enjoying their unique qualities.

I share emotional intimacy with my partner.

I want the best for my spouse and go out of my way to support them in their personal and professional life.

I am happy I am part of this family.

I enjoy activities and celebrations with my family.

I love my family even though they sometimes do not understand me.

I love my parents, my siblings, and my extended family unconditionally.

I show my family how much I love them in every way possible – both verbal and non-verbal.

My family provides the love and care I need.

All of my relationships are long-term and offer a positive, loving experience.

I am worthy of love and deserve to receive love in abundance.

I love those around me and I love myself. Others show me love.

I attract loving and caring people into my life.

My partner and I are both happy and in love. Our relationship is joyous.

I am thankful for the love in my life and I am thankful for my caring partner.

I only attract healthy, loving relationships.

I am with the love of my life. We both treat each other with respect.

I happily give and receive love each day.

I am so thankful for my partner and how caring they are.

Each day I am so grateful for how loved I am and much people care about me.

I know and trust that the Universe will only bring me loyal supporting and loving relationships.

I open my heart to love and know that I deserve it.

Wherever I go and whoever I am with, I find love.

I deserve to receive the love I get and I open myself to the love the Universe gives me.

I am open to marriage and attracting my future spouse.

My love grows stronger every day.

I am capable and deserving of a long lasting relationship.

My relationship will be open, honest and full of abundance.

Love surrounds me and everyone around me.

I am attracting my dream future.

I am confident, self-assured and full of charisma.

My partner is a reflection of me.

I will never give up on finding true love.

I exhale negativity and inhale happiness.

Today I will continue to create the foundation of a happy and loving relationship.

I love my soulmate and I love myself.

A happy partnership is supportive, balanced and affectionate.

I am manifesting my dream partner.

My relationships are always fulfilling.

I love being in a relationship.

Happiness begins with me and me alone. I have the power to create my own happiness.

I let go of my past relationships and look to the future.

I only think positively about love.

I am surrounded by love and everything is fine.

My heart is always open and I radiate love.

All my relationships are long lasting and loving.

I see everything with loving eyes and I love everything I see.

In life I always get what I give out and I always give out love.

I encounter love in all my relationships and I love these encounters.

I have attracted the most loving person in my life and life is now full of joy.

I love myself and everybody else and in return everybody loves me.

Everywhere I go, I find love. Life is joyous.

My partner is the love of my life and the center of my universe. He loves me as much as I love him.

I am surrounded by love and everything is fine.

My heart is always open and I radiate love.

All my relationships are long lasting and loving.

I see everything with loving eyes and I love everything I see.

My partner is the love of my life and the center of my universe. He loves me as much as I love him.

In life, I always get what I give out and I always give out love.

I encounter love in all my relationships and I love these encounters.

I deserve love and I get it in abundance.

I have attracted the most loving person in my life and life is now full of joy.

I love myself and everybody else and in return everybody loves me.

Everywhere I go, I find love. Life is joyous.

My partner and I are the perfect matches for each other and the love between us is divine.

Whatever be my relationship, love and forgiveness is the foundation of that relationship.

In all my relationships, with my parents, siblings, my life partner or my friends, I only give love and seek love.

The grass is never greener on the other side; it's greener where I water and tend to it.

My partner is a reflection of me.

I look inward for all the answers to my problems.

I accept responsibility for my actions and make right my wrongs.

I am forgiving.

I will never give up on love.

Energy spent loving is never a loss.

The light in me sees the light in you.

My love is unconditional.

Separateness is an illusion; my partner and I are one.

I am worthy of love and deserve to be loved unconditionally.

I treat my partner the way I want to be treated.

My partner is loving, generous and kind.

I attract exactly what I need in my relationship.

I express love in various forms.

I am open to love in all forms.

I am open, free and joyful.

My partner loves and appreciates me.

I feel safe and protected by my partner.

I look at my partner through my eyes via my heart.

I have a twinkle in my eye for my partner.

I focus on the good in everything.

I listen with an open heart and a loving ear.

I put my best foot forward in my relationship.

No one is perfect, including me.

If someone pushes my buttons, they are still MY buttons – personal issues I need to tend to.

I am understanding.

My goal is always to create harmony and clarity.

I listen to understand and not to "win."

No one ever wins in an argument.

I communicate in peace and with compassion.

I remain in balance with my emotions.

I practice patience with grace and ease.

I am flexible.

I create the foundation on which my relationship is built.

I do the best I can.

I'm either destroying or building in every moment.

I am honest, trustworthy and truthful.

I am trusting in my relationship.

I accept my partner's flaws and always leave room for growth.

I support my partner's dreams.

With every action, I am being an example of what I want to see in my partner.

I avoid blaming and pointing the finger.

I speak only kind words about my partner.

I never complain.

I state my needs clearly and honestly.

I speak my truth without blame or shame.

I always leave the door open for affection.

I never give my partner the cold shoulder and continually hold space for change.

I set the space and tone for love to express itself.

Loving my partner is loving myself.

I am a warrior for love.

I create a sanctuary in my home that is always inviting to my partner.

I stand firm and grounded in love.

Love emanates from my very being and affects all around me.

No one can hurt me, for I am the only one that can hurt myself.

I think positively of my partner.

I encourage my partner to reach for the stars.

I let go of all grudges and resentment.

I don't bring up old wounds.

My energy transforms conflict into oneness and unity.

I always leave room for improvement.

Through intention, I achieve my ideal relationship.

I cannot change anyone else, I can only change myself.

Happiness starts within.

I am content and joyful alone and my partner only adds on to the good feeling that's already there.

I T.H.I.N.K. before I speak:

I love myself, I love all the people around me, I love the entire world

I am a unique, special and loving human being, constantly attracting pleasant and kind people in my life

I am deeply grateful for all the people I love and for all the people who love me

Every day, everywhere I go, and in everything I do, love is in and around me

The love that I feel for my family and myself cannot be described with words

My soul mate loves me very much for what I am eternally happy and deeply grateful

I am a peaceful, pleasant human being filled with love and shiny light

I am very proud of all my accomplishments

I respect and love myself, therefore, everyone around me receives that energy and in turn respects and loves me

I would give anything for the people I love and they would give anything for me

I know that I deserve to be loved so I am open and ready to receive it

I attract relationships to me that are for the highest good of all.

I love sharing amazing conversations with my friends, family and lover.

I enjoy and thrive in the company of great friends.

I love laughing and having fun in my relationships.

I love that my relationships are in harmony with my highest good.

I accept that I am loved and treasured for who I really AM.

I give and receive love freely and fully in all my relationships.

I love being supported by my friends, family, and relationships.

I enjoy sharing the real me in relationships.

I know with every fiber of my being that the Universe is bringing me only the most supportive, loving, and awesome relationships!

I love that my marriage is becoming deeper, stronger, and more loving every day.

My spouse loves and accepts me just as I am.

I thrive and enjoy being in a loving, supportive, and happy marriage.

I feel safe and secure with my partner.

I adore being loved and wanted by my partner.

I accept that a warm, loving, committed marriage is mine right now.

I love loving and being loved by my mate.

I enjoy being loved and treasured by my amazing, kind, and generous partner.

I accept perfect divine love right now.

I go through life knowing how loved I am.

A river of romance fills my life with love and joy.

I love that my relationship is becoming more romantic every day.

I enjoy how my partner showers me with romance.

I find romance everywhere I go.

I let my partner surprise and delight me with romance.

I love filling my relationship with romance.

I give and receive romance freely and happily.

I accept that I can receive romance right now.

I am open to receiving more romance in my life.

I love romance and romance loves me.

There is a deep understanding between my partner and I.

Forgiveness and compassion is the foundation of my romantic relationship.

It is easy for me to look in the mirror and say, "I love you."

My words are always kind and loving, and in return, I hear kindness and love from others.

Every day of my life is filled with love.

All communication between my partner and I is loving and kind.

I know that I am of good health.

My heart is always open and I radiate love.

My business is an all-consuming love affair and I attract whatever I need through it.

I am prosperous, healthy, and happy and I live in abundance.

I open myself to the beauty, joy, and harmony of the Universe and I enjoy it.

I love and respect myself at all times

My heart is open to love.

There are no failures. I learn from everything I do.

I believe that everything is for my highest good and greatest joy.

I move beyond forgiveness, to understanding, and I have compassion and kindness for myself and others.

I see everything with loving eyes and I love everything I see.

I forgive those who need forgiving, for not being what I wanted them to be.

I deserve love and I get it in abundance.

I will speak easily and truthfully to myself and others.

I am a good listener.

I attract love in everything that I do.

I am a good communicator.

I allow love to find me easily and effortlessly.

I am calm.

I love and trust my creative gifts.

I welcome love with open arms.

I accept that I am an unlimited being and that I can create anything I want.

I am open to new ideas, people, and situations which will enhance my joy and happiness.

The more love I give the more there is to receive.

I am open to the goodness and abundance of the Universe.

Everything about me is lovable and worthy of love.

I am with my soulmate because I am a loving, kind person who deserves true love.

I wake up every morning filled with joy, because I know that I face each day with the support and love of my partner.

All of my relationships are healthy because they are based in love and compassion

I radiate love and others reflect love back to me.

I am loving and lovable.

I am attractive.

My romantic relationship is healthy, long-lasting and full of love.

My partner is kind, compassionate and understanding.

My partner is very physically and spiritually attracted to me.

I am with my soulmate and we share a life full of love.

Life is full of love and I find it everywhere I go.

My relationship is divine, and my partner and I are perfectly matched

All of my relationships are long-term and offer a positive, loving experience.

I am worthy of love and deserve to receive love in abundance.

I love those around me and I love myself. Others show me love.

I attract loving and caring people into my life.

My partner and I are both happy and in love. Our relationship is joyous.

I am thankful for the love in my life and I am thankful for my caring partner.

I only attract healthy, loving relationships.

I am with the love of my life. We both treat each other with respect.

I happily give and receive love each day.

I am so thankful for my partner and how caring they are.

Each day I am so grateful for how loved I am and much people care about me.

I know and trust that the Universe will only bring me loyal supporting and loving relationships.

I open my heart to love and know that I deserve it.

Wherever I go and whoever I am with, I find love.

I deserve to receive the love I get and I open myself to the love the Universe gives me.

I am open to marriage and attracting my future spouse.

I am capable and deserving of a long lasting relationship.

My relationship will be open, honest and full of abundance.

Love surrounds me and everyone around me.

I am attracting my dream future.

I am confident, self-assured and full of charisma.

My partner is a reflection of me.

I will never give up on finding true love.

I exhale negativity and inhale happiness.

Today I will continue to create the foundation of a happy and loving relationship.

I love my soulmate and I love myself.

A happy partnership is supportive, balanced and affectionate.

I am manifesting my dream partner.

My relationships are always fulfilling.

I love being in a relationship.

Happiness begins with me and me alone. I have the power to create my own happiness.

I let go of my past relationships and look to the future.

I only think positively about love.

I am surrounded by love and everything is fine.

My heart is always open and

I radiate love.

ABUNDANCE AFFIRMATION

I am grateful for the abundance that flows to me daily.

My actions draw abundance to me in all that I do.

The Lord gives me more than I need and I am grateful.

I am easily and openly accepting the abundance that is inherently mine.

I live in abundance.

I am now claiming the abundance that is rightfully mine.

Abundance comes easily to me.

I choose to be financially abundant in my life.

I am passionate about building a life of abundance in all areas.

Being abundant is my birthright. And I claim it now.

I am abundant in all areas of my life.

Abundance is flowing to me now.

I naturally attract abundance into my life.

I have great abundance and share it freely with those around me.

Everything I touch returns abundantly to me.

I am abundantly happy.

I have an abundance of friends that surround me.

My career path is abundant.

I have an abundant number of people in my life that inspire and uplift me.

I am abundant in my faith.

I am abundantly happy.

Abundance and joy flow freely in my life.

Abundance is naturally mine.

Abundance is attracted to me.

I attract abundance in all that I am and do.

Money flows to me easily and abundantly

Everything I need is coming to me easily and effortlessly

I am capable of creating financial abundance.

Having all the money I need is possible for me and I deserve it.

I am a living magnet for financial abundance and wealth in all its forms

I am aware that I am an individualized expression of the infinite flow of love, creativity and abundance. Money flows to me from all directions

I feel prosperous at all times

I give and receive money freely

Everything I need is already within me

I now have the time, energy wisdom and money to accomplish all my desires

It is okay for me to have everything I want

This is a rich universe with plenty for all

I now have a perfectly satisfying, well paying job

I love my work and I am well rewarded for the service I provide

. I have the ability to create anything that I want.

My life is filled with great abundance in every area.

I accept and allow success in all areas of my life.

I firmly believe in my ability to attract success.

Great things are coming to me today.

I attract everything that I desire.

I am totally committed to achieve my goals and dreams.

Money comes to me easily and effortlessly.

All good things flow into my life.

I am a Powerful Money Magnet.

I attract success into my life effortlessly.

I am open and ready to attract abundance into my life.

I am a magnet for financial abundance and prosperity.

I am attracting positive and abundant people into my life.

I am positive, passionate and successful.

I learn from the past, live in the present and plan for the future.

I easily attract the things that I desire most.

My positive belief in myself is transforming my life.

My dreams are manifesting before my eyes.

I am filled with limitless potential.

I AM worthy of love, abundance, success, happiness and fulfilment.

Abundance surrounds me everywhere I go.

I rejoice in others success, wealth, and prosperity.

Everyday I turn my dreams into reality.

I have the power to manifest wealth and abundance in my life.

The power to be successful is within me.

Everything I need for success comes to me easily and effortlessly.

Every day I attract people who help me achieve my goals.

I am Living the Life of my Dreams.

Money flows easily into my life

I am open to receive abundant gifts from God.

I am open to all possibilities for abundance.

I accept the abundance the universe gives me.

I am open to receive something wonderful today.

I receive prosperity without limits.

I feel prosperous.

I am a source of abundance.

God's abundance manifests through me.

There is plenty of money in the Universe, and there is plenty for me.

My mind is constantly attracting money into my life.

My mind is in harmony with the energies that create abundance.

I am attracting into my life opportunities for making money.

Each day, I am getting more comfortable about the idea of having a lot of money.

I am getting used to the idea of being wealthy.

I am confident that the Universe is helping me get all the money I need, and even more.

If other people achieved success, I can too.

My bank manager always welcomes me with a big smile.

Piles of money are piling up in my bank account.

I have a great job with a wonderful salary.

My financial situation is improving beyond my dreams.

My business is attracting a lot of paying customers.

Money is appearing in my life through many channels, and in harmonious ways.

You don't want to – you're perfectly happy with your state of finances.

You don't think you deserve it even though you'd never admit this.

You don't think it's possible given your life's situation.

You think rich is evil and poverty is noble.

You think money will make you do bad things.

You feel torn, guilty and conflicted about your desire to be wealthy and prosperous.

You blame your parents for not having enough money and not teaching you better.

You believe riches are bestowed upon a lucky few.

You think you will be unhappy because money isn't supposed to buy happiness.

You think the only way to be wealthy is if you married into wealth or came of wealth.

You have none of these self-limiting beliefs; you just have no idea how to make more money yet you won't seek expert advice.

My passion is the key to my abundance.

Wealth is pouring into my life.

I am getting wealthier each day.

I enjoy travel whenever I please.

I am successful in whatever I do.

I am constantly adding to my income.

I always have enough money for all that I need.

I am getting wealthier each day.

I am wealthy beyond my fondest dreams.

The universe brings me fulfillment and abundance.

Everything I touch is a success.

Money flows to me easily, frequently and abundantly.

I use money to make the world a better place.

I enjoy multiple streams of passive income.

I enjoy an abundance of money.

I clearly see opportunities to make money effortlessly.

I feel great about loving money.

Money loves me; I now have more than I need

I enjoy abundance in all areas of my life

Today is filled with opportunity, and I will seize it.

Being wealthy gives me joy, happiness and peace of mind.

I am now free to do the things I love.

Everything good is coming to me easily and effortlessly.

Thank you Universe for my great abundance.

Feeling joyful attracts abundance.

I allow all good things to come into my life, and I enjoy them.

Wealth is a positive expression of divine energy.

I can easily imagine myself having limitless abundance.

Money always flows to me easily.

I realize that I can help others with my wealth; so I stay wealthy.

I am prosperous in everything I do.

I am thankful for the abundance and prosperity in my life.

Abundance around me, abundance within me, abundance throughout me.

All my needs are met instantaneously.

I know there is ample prosperity for all.

I have the power to be successful.

I allow my passions to perpetuate good in the world through my wealth.

I let go of all resistance to prosperity, and it comes to me naturally.

I am magnetic to money, and it is magnetic to me.

Prosperity now happens to me.

Money flows freely in my life.

I am relaxing into greater abundance.

I now release the goldmine within me.

I am worthy of receiving prosperity now.

I am willing to be more abundant now.

I am now accumulating large sums of money.

Like a powerful magnet, I attract all my desires in great abundance.

I release all opposition to wealth.

I am certain that my path is always perfect for me.

I am abundant.

Abundance is my divine birthright.

Prosperity and abundance surround me.

I release all negativity around building wealth.

I attract prosperity with each thought I think.

I am extremely successful.

I deserve the best and it comes to me now.

I enjoy my prosperity, and share it freely with the world.

Everything and everybody prospers me now.

Abundance and prosperity are my birthright and I accept it with open arms.

Prosperity and abundance are in my blood.

Prosperity is abundantly mine

I live in prosperity and abundance.

Prosperity flows abundantly into my life

My life overflows with abundance and prosperity

Prosperity is abundant in my life

Abundant prosperity is naturally attracted to me

I am abundantly prosperous

Prosperity is abundant in my life

I am grateful for the prosperity that flows to me daily.

I see myself Prosperous and that is who I am.

Prosperity surrounds me and I share it freely with the world

I give freely from my prosperity

My life overflows with abundance and prosperity

Prosperity is abundant in my life

My prosperity grows more and more every day.

I deserve to have financial abundance and prosperity in my life now

My actions draw prosperity to me in all that I do.

The Lord gives me more than I need and I am grateful.

I am easily and openly accepting the prosperity that is inherently mine.

I live in prosperity.

I am now claiming the prosperity and wealth that is rightfully mine.

I create wealth and prosperity easily and effortlessly.

My prosperity is limitless.

I expect wealth, abundance, wealth and prosperity in my life everyday.

Prosperity comes easily to me.

I choose to be financially prosperous in my life.

I have unlimited prosperity

I am grateful for my over abundant prosperity.

Prosperity allows me the freedom to do as I wish

I am passionate about building a life of prosperity.

Being prosperous is my birthright. And I claim it now.

I am prosperous in all areas of my life.

Prosperity is flowing to me now.

Abundant prosperity is naturally attracted to me

I am abundantly prosperous

Prosperity is abundant in my life

Prosperity is abundantly mine

I live in prosperity and abundance.

Prosperity flows abundantly into my life

I welcome the prosperity that is inherently mine.

I naturally attract prosperity and wealth into my life.

I have great prosperity and share it freely with those around me.

Everything I touch returns prosperously to me.

I enjoy prosperity in all areas of my life

I am prosperous and happy

I give thanks that the prosperity which is mine by design and pours in and piles up under grace in perfect ways.

I have prosperity in all that I do

My career path is prosperous

Abundance and prosperity are my birthright and I accept it with open arms.

Prosperity and abundance are in my blood.

I surround myself with prosperity

I am prosperous in my faith

Prosperity and joy flow freely in my life

Prosperity is naturally mine

Prosperity is attracted to me

I attract prosperity in all that I am and do

I can and will have more than I ever dreamed possible.

I feel good about money and deserve it in my life.

Great wealth is flowing to me now.

I now create my wonderful, ideal life.

I am thankful for the comfort and joy that money provides me.

I know I am abundant.

I always have enough money for myself.

Every day in every way I am becoming more and more prosperous.

I see myself as wealthy, and that's who I am.

I choose wealth and abundance.

My wealth derives from honesty in everything I do.

I am worthy of great success.

My greatest good is coming to me now.

I love abundance in all its beautiful forms.

I am wide awake to my abundance.

I release all my negative beliefs about money and invite wealth into my life.

I am prosperous, healthy, happy and live in abundance.

Wealth is my birth-right, my natural state of being.

Making money is good for me and for everyone in my life.

My income is growing higher and higher now.

Money is an important part of my life and is never away from me.

All my issues with wealth have disappeared.

I clearly see opportunities to effortlessly make money.

I am wealthy.

Whatever I do, it always ends in amassing wealth.

I attract prosperity.

Money flows freely and abundantly into my life.

I will be productive and prosperous today

My prosperity is unlimited, my success is unlimited now.

I always have whatever I need.

Perfect abundance is my chosen reality.

Money comes to me easily and effortlessly.

Every day in every way, my wealth is increasing.

I am destined to find prosperity in everything I do.

I am gracious for the wealth I have in my life.

I am free to do whatever I wish to do.

My riches are forever increasing as I give more of myself in service to the world

I radiate wealth, abundance, and prosperity

Riches flow through me like waves in the ocean and come back again.

I only think thoughts of wealth and abundance.

I am a wealthy entrepreneur who is living life on my own terms.

I release every block that held me back from receiving prosperity.

Wealth flows to me from all directions.

I'm financially abundant, and money comes to me naturally.

I allow myself to be drenched with financial abundance always, and I generously share my wealth

Today I am attracting wealth, abundance, and wellbeing.

My wallet and bank balance is overflowing with money.

My wealth shines from within me.

I create an avalanche of financial abundance, and I give back in amazing ways

I feel marvelous as a rich person.

Wealth is pouring into my life.

Large amounts of money are coming to me in ever increasing amounts.

I am grateful for everything that I receive

Wealth floats around me daily.

My life is full of abundance."

"Money comes to me easily and effortlessly."

I am increasingly magnetic to health, wealth, abundance, prosperity, and money."

"Every day I am attracting more and more abundance into my life.

I am a success magnet."

My life is full of unlimited abundance."

I am open and ready to attract abundance into my life."

I am abundance."

"I am attuned to the frequency of love and abundance."

I am wealthy."

I attract success."

I am open to receiving limitless abundance."

I see abundance all around me."

I have an abundance mindset."

I am living my life in a state of complete abundance."

"I radiate abundance."

"I am living a life of abundance."

I am worthy of all my heart desires.

I always have all I need when I need it.

Miracles and magic surround me wherever I go. My brand is full of miracles.

My brand is filled with joyous success and rich abundance.

I have abundance to share.

I share my gifts with others.

I am surrounded by abundance.

I make meaningful contributions to society.

My world is filled with abundance of health, wealth and happiness.

Abundance surrounds me, today I claim my share. My brand is mine to create.

Money flows freely and abundantly into my life. I love having a prosperous brand and career.

Success and money come easy to me.

I get everything that I desire by first helping others get everything they desire.

I love my work and my work energizes me.

Success and growth are inevitable outcomes of my work.

I picture myself with abundance for others.

I am surrounded by people who are eager to contribute to my abundance.

I appreciate everything I have, and therefore I manifest more abundance.

I am successful right now.

I invest in myself and my business every day. I appreciate all the lessons owning a business has taught me

Everyday I am becoming richer and richer

Money comes to me easily and effortlessly.

Wealth constantly flows into my life.

My actions create constant wealth, prosperity, and abundance.

I am aligned with the energy of wealth and abundance.

I am a magnet for money.

Prosperity is drawn to me.

I have a wealth mindset.

I'm open and receptive to all the wealth life offers me.

I am wealthy.

I always have more than enough money.

I attract money to me.

HEALTHY BRAIN AFFIRMATION

I find it easier and easier each day to let go and just be.

I am, I can, I will.

My body is a temple of everything good and it reflects that good.

Every day I am letting go and allowing love to flow through my body.

Every day I grow stronger in mind, body and soul.

Today I begin a new life, restored and renewed.

My positive thoughts and actions renew my mind and body.

Today I release all and any illness, I bless it for it's lessons and I move on to health and abundance.

As I grow in spiritual consciousness, my health is renewed.

My body is my home and it represents all the good that is me.

I radiate good health.

I have all the energy I need to accomplish my goals.

My body is healed, restored and filled with energy.

Day by day, I am growing healthier and stronger.

I love and care for my body and it cares for me.

I am healthy, fit and active.

I am creating healing energy in my life and in my body.

I am living a long and healthy life.

I feel good and my body feels good.

I am active, energetic and in control of my life

I believe in my dreams. Believe in yourself and all that you are. ...

I am doing my best every day. ...

I love myself for who I am. ...

I am in charge of my own happiness. ...

I accept 100% responsibility for my own life. ...

The best is yet to come. ...

I am grateful for every day.

I trust my life is divinely guided.

I trust the outcomes in my life are for the best.

I trust that all that I need comes to me when needed.

I feel safe trusting God in my life.

I trust I am exactly where I am supposed to be now.

I can trust life.

I am in harmony with divine guidance.

I automatically live in trust.

I trust that everything works for the highest good.

I am confident of my future.

I am confident, enthusiastic, and energetic.

and my personality shows I am confident.

I attract confident people.

I breath in and out, exhaling hesitancy and inhaling confidence.

I love change, easily adjusting to new people and situation.

I love meeting strangers and approach them with boldness and enthusiasm.

I thrive on self-confidence, knowing that nothing is impossible.

I am outgoing and make friends easily.

I am a unique individual, with many special talents and abilities.

I am attractive, healthy, and confident.

I am happy with myself the way I am.

I am proud of myself and the things I have accomplished.

I am worthy of great things in my life.

I like myself just the way I am.

My self-esteem and confidence increases each day.

All of my thoughts and feelings are under control.

I awake each day with excitement, awaiting the good things coming to me.

I breathe in and out, releasing all stress from my body.

I forgive myself for mistakes and bad decisions I have made.

I observe my emotions without overreacting.

I meditate with joy and without resistance or anxiety.

I reject the idea that I am a prisoner of my emotions and past actions.

Every day, in every way, I am getting healthier and healthier.

I eat healthy and I stay healthy.

Every day my eyesight is better than the previous day.

I get good sleep every night and I get up fresh every morning.

I love exercising and I exercise every day.

I am grateful for my healthy body and I bless every part of my body.

Perfect health is my divine right and I claim it now.

Every cell in my body is healthy and radiates health.

My immune system is very strong and can deal with any kind of bacteria, germs and viruses.

Every organ in my body is healthy and functions at its optimum scale.

I am pain free in every respect and my body is full of energy.

Throughout the day I am full of energy.

I breathe deeply and every breath energizes me.

I love myself in totality and I radiate energy.

My body metabolism is at its optimum and provides me with all the energy that I need

They reinforce your goals and help you achieve them.

They motivate you to take positive, forward-moving action in your daily activities.

They allow you to focus more on positive thoughts than self-defeating thoughts.

They help relieve stress and anxiety.

They foster mental clarity and focus.

They help build stronger, more intimate relationships.

They improve feelings of gratitude, appreciation, and general happiness.

They work in tandem with other mindfulness activities like meditation and present moment awareness.

Happiness is my birthright. I embrace happiness as my setpoint state of being.

I feel joy and contentment at this moment right now.

I awaken in the morning feeling happy and enthusiastic about life

I can tap into a wellspring of inner happiness anytime I wish.

By allowing myself to be happy, I inspire others to be happy as well.

I have fun with all of my endeavors, even the most mundane.

I look at the world around me and can't help but smile and feel joy.

I find joy and pleasure in the most simple things in life.

I have an active sense of humor and love to share laughter with others.

My heart is overflowing with joy.

I rest in happiness when I go to sleep, knowing all is well in my world.

When I breathe, I inhale confidence and exhale timidity.

I love meeting strangers and approach them with boldness and enthusiasm.

I live in the present and am confident of the future.

My personality exudes confidence. I am bold and outgoing.

I am self-reliant, creative and persistent in whatever I do.

I am energetic and enthusiastic. Confidence is my second nature

I am a problem solver. I focus on solutions and always find the best solution.

I love change and easily adjust myself to new situations.

I am well groomed, healthy and full of confidence. My outer self is matched by my inner well being.

Self-confidence is what I thrive on. Nothing is impossible and life is great.

I always see only the good in others. I attract only positive confident people.

Every cell in my body vibrates with energy and health.

I observe my emotions without getting attached to them.

I nourish my body with healthy food.

All of my body systems are functioning perfectly.

My body is healing, and I feel better and better every day.

I enjoy exercising my body and strengthening my muscles.

With every breath out, I release stress in my body.

I send love and healing to every organ of my body.

I breathe deeply, exercise regularly and feed only good nutritious food to my body.

Calmness washes over me with every deep breath I take.

I meditate easily without resistance or anxiety.

Being calm and relaxed energizes my whole being.

All the muscles in my body are releasing and relaxing.

All negativity and stress are evaporating from my body and my mind.

I breathe in relaxation. I breathe out stress. Even when there is chaos around me, I remain calm and centered.

I transcend stress of any kind. I live in peace.

I gently and easily return to the present moment.

All is well in my world. I am calm, happy, and content

Improve concentration

Relax and sleep well

Build self confidence

Accelerate learning of skills

Deal with fear and negativity

Heal quickly from sickness or injury

Increase endurance, strength, and performance

Train faster and more efficiently

Improve relationships

Improve quality of life and wellbeing

I am healthy, happy and radiant.

I appreciate and love my body

I love feeling fit and strong. It is easy for me to eat well and exercise regularly

The older I get the healthier I become

I radiate good health.

I am calm and at peace

I am focused and motivated

My sleep is relaxed and refreshing.

I have all the energy I need to accomplish my goals.

My body is healed, restored and filled with energy.

I have abundant energy, vitality and well-being.

My body maintains its ideal weight and health

I am filled with energy for all the daily activities in my life.

My mind is at peace.

I choose to be at a healthy weight

Every day, in every way, I am becoming better and better.

I am healthy and happy.

I love and care for my body and it cares for me.

I create a safe and secure space for myself wherever I am.

I give myself permission to do what is right for me.

I am confident in my ability to [fill in the blank].

I use my time and talents to help others [fill in the blank].

What I love about myself is my ability to [fill in the blank].

I feel proud of myself when I [fill in the blank].

I give myself space to grow and learn.

I allow myself to be who I am without judgment.

I listen to my intuition and trust my inner guide.

I accept my emotions and let them serve their purpose.

I give myself the care and attention that I deserve.

My drive and ambition allow me to achieve my goals.

I share my talents with the world by [fill in the blank].

I am good at helping others to [fill in the blank].

I am always headed in the right direction.

I trust that I am on the right path.

I am creatively inspired by the world around me.

My mind is full of brilliant ideas.

I put my energy into things that matter to me.

I trust myself to make the right decision.

I am becoming closer to my true self every day.

I am grateful to have people in my life who [fill in the blank].

I am learning valuable lessons from myself every day.

I am at peace with who I am as a person.

I make a difference in the world by simply existing in it.

I am my own version of beautiful, which no-one else can be

I am confident in my individuality

I am enough

I am worthy of love, success and happiness

I love myself. I believe in myself. I support myself

I honor my own life path

I give myself permission to be well

My every step is one of courage

I am supported and loved in this healing journey of mine

I have come this far and I can keep going

I am powerful, confident, and capable of reaching all my dreams

Every day is a new day full of hope, happiness and health

Every day in every way I am getting healthier and healthier and feeling better and better

I accept and embrace my imperfections

I am taking care of myself today

My self care is worth making time for

I am choosing to be happy

I know what I value and place my energy there

I am safe

My life is just beginning

I am talented and have many things to offer

I choose to make the rest of my life the best of my life

I am excited that my actions are improving my life

I make a difference

Today I have unlimited confidence in my abilities

I am rich with creative ideas

I am independent in my thinking. I choose thoughts that make me feel free

My perfect career opportunity is right around the corner

I enjoy making others laugh

I'm an excellent listener

- I am in charge of my thoughts, I have a positive mindset

- I already possess all the qualities needed to be successful
- My body is healthy, my mind is knowledgeable, my heart is serene
- I choose happiness and am grateful for the blessings of health, love and family
- I am brave and stand up for what I believe in
- I am a highly regarded employee
- My body is healthy and I only eat nourishing food
- I am loving and worthy of love
- I am forgiving and compassionate towards others
- I am excited about every day of my life
- I accomplish all my goals with ease
- I am in control of how I react to others
- I deserve to have Joy in my life
- I am happy, calm and at peace. All is well in my world
- I am allowed to make mistakes, mistakes teach me worthwhile lessons
- I am worthy of respect
- My contributions to the world are valuable
- I am enough, just as I am
- I am in charge of my life and the path it takes
- I am beautiful and unique

- I am blessed with amazing family and friends
- I am open to new adventures and ideas
- I am in charge of my thoughts, I have a positive mindset
- I already possess all the qualities needed to be successful
- My body is healthy, my mind is knowledgeable, my heart is serene
- I choose happiness and am grateful for the blessings of health, love and family
- I am brave and stand up for what I believe in
- I am a highly regarded employee
- My body is healthy and I only eat nourishing food
- I am loving and worthy of love
- I am forgiving and compassionate towards others
- I am excited about every day of my life
- I accomplish all my goals with ease
- I awake each day filled with happiness
- I find solutions to challenges and move past them calmly
- I attract the best circumstances and people in my life
- I love change and adapt to new situations easily
- I am proud of myself and all that I do
- I am secure in who I am
- I inhale calm and exhale tension

- I listen to my body and give it what it needs

- My home is a peaceful place where I am safe and happy

- I am grateful for this present moment and find joy in it

- I choose the life I want. I am happy, successful and confident even as I work towards more success, greater joy and personal development in my life.

  o   Today, I make smart decisions.

  o   I greet the day with joy and gratitude.

  o   I am so grateful for another day on this Earth; thank you!

  o   Today is going to be great because I will make it so.

  o   This is the day the Lord has made; let us rejoice and be glad in it.

  o   My day is off to a positive start.

  o   Hello, World! Here I come.

  o   Today I live a purpose-filled life.

  o   I share my full potential with those around me.

  o   I am energized and strong.

  o   Wellness and abundance are flowing into my life.

  o   I see new opportunities all around me.

  o   Positive mind, positive life.

  o   I'm awake to the possibilities around me.

  o   Divine energy surrounds me.

- Today I choose happiness and wellbeing.
- Something wonderful will happen today.
- I was put here to achieve my greatest self.
- Today, I am blessed.
- "Mine is the sunlight, mine is the morning."
- Everything is good right now.
- I accept and embrace all of life's experiences, even the unpleasant ones.
- I am completely in control of my thoughts.
- I am participating in the experiences of the moment.
- I easily return to the present moment and what is happening to me.
- I find joy in the moment.
- I remain engaged and focused on the present moment.

HAPPINESS AFFIRMATION

I have the power to shape my ideal reality

I create the life I desire with my good feelings

Everything is always working out well for me

When I feel happy I manifest more reasons to be happy

I look at the world around me, I feel joy and smile.

I am happy as I pursue my daily tasks.

I am happy.

I embrace happiness as my way of looking at the world.

I feel happy and content in this moment right now.

I have inner happiness that I can tap into anytime I want to.

I love to laugh and find humor in everyday situations.

I wake up in the morning feeling happy about my life.

My happiness inspires those around me to be happy,

Things are getting better every day.

I am willing to be happy now

I accept that happiness is my true nature

I am worthy of feeling happy

I am important to others – my family and my friends.

I feel the love of both those who are close to me and those not physically around me.

I love, like, and approve of myself.

I release past anger, hurts, and loneliness, filling myself joy.

I take pleasure in being alone.

I choose to be happy and grateful today.

Happiness flows through me constantly.

My future is full of light and laughter.

There are amazing things in my life; no matter how small they may seem, they are significant.

I am at peace with my past.

I am loved by others as much as I love them.

I am overwhelmed by feeling of for my life and everyone in it.

I am surrounded by love.

I great each moment of each day with love.

I radiate love and happiness.

My happiness comes from within me

I create my happiness by accepting every part of myself with unconditional love

Joy is the essence of my being

I see so many positives in my life

I am constantly creating everything my heart desires

I experience joy in everything I do

I feel happy with myself as a person

I give myself permission to enjoy myself

I allow myself to feel good

The life I've always dreamed of is created by my choice to be joyful now

Following my joy reveals the path to my best life

My choice to be happy keeps me in perfect health

The happiness I feel is felt by everyone around me

I create the possibility of happiness for others by being happy

I am meant to live a happy life

My inner joy expands when I share it with others

All the good in my life comes to me as result of my willingness to find happiness in each moment

My happiness is reflected back to me in everything I attract.

My inner joy is the source of all the good in my life

I am the happiest person on the planet

I am aware that all happiness comes from inside so I live every moment to the fullest

I can find happiness in the small things and I know that all I need in order to be happy are my thoughts and my feelings

The purpose of my life is to be happy and to give happiness to all the people I love

I am waking up every single day with a smile on my face being grateful for all the happy moments that are awaiting for me

I give and receive love freely and joyfully.

I find love everywhere I go. Life is amazing!

I love being with people who bring out the best in me.

I see myself as being filled with love and happiness.

I feel like I matter. I am a contribution to this world.

I accept that I don't have to do anything to be loved and happy.

I love myself totally.

I accept that I can receive love and happiness right now!

I accept that I am infinitely loved.

I am loved. I am loved. I am loved!

I experience joy in everything I do

I forgive myself

What I did is in the past and now I can create my future

I forgive everyone that has hurt me in the past and move forward with a cleansed soul

I forgive those who have harmed me in my past and peacefully detach from them

I live a positive life and only attract the best in my life

I am peacefully allowing my life to unfold

Today, and every day, I choose to be happy

I am fun and energetic and people love me for it

My life overflows with happiness and love

I always have everything I need to be happy

I fuel my mind with healthy thoughts

Every day in every way I am getting happier and happier.

Happiness is my birth right. I choose to be happy and I deserve to be happy.

Every new day starts with happiness,

is full of joy and ends with contentment.

Happiness is contagious. I spread happiness to others and absorb happiness from others.

I touch many lives. My happiness makes all these people happy, thus making it one big happy world.

My happy disposition attracts happiness into my life. I interact only with happy people and have only happy experiences.

The whole process of living makes me happy. Moving towards my goal makes me happy.

I am grateful to God for this wonderful life. I am thankful to every body who has touched my life and made it worth living.

I enjoy every moment of the day.

Be happy is my motto.

Being happy comes easy to me.

Happiness is my second nature.

Happy thoughts come to me naturally. I always land in happy circumstances.

The future is always bright and happy. I look at only the bright side of things.

I perform my random act of kindness regularly. Kindness breeds love and love results in happiness.

For me, happiness is a journey, not a destination. God has blessed me with happiness and my journey is endless.

I am kind, I am loving, I am happy.

I deserve to be healthy, happy, and successful.

I'm good with who I am, I'm proud of who I'm becoming.

I'm committing myself to live a happy life.

I don't need to show off to prove that I'm doing well.

I am Happy.

I'm creating the life I deserve to live.

I don't need to live life in a way that will impress others. I need to live my life in a way that will keep me happy.

I'm going to accomplish all of my dreams. I'm going to think, speak and work them into existence.

I'm not selfish if I focus on myself for a little bit. I need to make sure I'm okay and happy.

I will choose the happiness of this moment, instead of the pain of the past.

I am a radiant and joyous person.

People hating on me will not stop my happiness.

I am good at loving others and I make others happy.

The only person I want to be is a better version of myself.

I'm going to reach every goal I set for myself. I'm not giving up on any of my dreams.

Happiness and love flow freely from me.

Every day in every way I am getting happier and happier.

I am surrounded by loving people, cuddly creatures, and happy plants.

I am open to laughter today.

When I can control how I feel, I can control my future.

I'm making the conscious, continued effort to heal and be happy. It's great.

I choose to be happy.

I want to be happy rather than looking happy.

I give myself permission to be happy.

I'm proud of my self because the work I did today got me a little bit closer to living my dreams.

I am allowing myself to be consistently and genuinely happy.

An angel like me doesn't deserve all this sadness.

I am worthy of feeling happy all day, every day.39. It is possible for me to feel happy all day, every day.

I am allowing myself to feel happy all day, every day.

It is natural for me to feel happy all day, every day.

It is easy for me to feel happy all day, every day.

I am attracting and allowing money to come to me in ways that will make me really, really happy.

I am unique; I feel great about being alive & being me.

Amazing opportunities exist for me in every aspect of my life.

I deserve all of the good things that are in my life.

I'm able to be happy for people that aren't in my life anymore when I see them doing well.

I choose to create a happy life.

I choose to focus on things that feel good.

I attract a loving happy family for myself.

Powerful subliminal

I am happy

I think only positive thoughts

I am 100% happy with who I am

I am able to see the good in every situation

I cannot do this.

I am too lazy.

I lack inner strength.

I am going to fail.

I am healthy and happy.

Wealth is pouring into my life.

I am sailing on the river of wealth.

I am getting wealthier each day.

My body is healthy and functioning in a very good way.

I have a lot of energy.

I study and comprehend fast.

My mind is calm.

I am calm and relaxed in every situation.

I am at peace with myself and the world.

I forgive myself for all the mistakes I have done.

My thoughts are under my control.

I radiate love and happiness.

I am surrounded by love.

I have the perfect job for me.

I am living in the house of my dreams.

I have a wonderful and satisfying job.

I have the means to travel abroad, whenever I want to.

I am successful in whatever I do.

Everything is getting better every day.

My mind is filled with positivity and my life is full with joy.

I think positive thoughts that attract happiness and prosperity into my life.

My efforts are fruitful, and all my plans turn out even better than I expected. I have plenty of inspiration, motivation and courage, which help me achieve everything i want

I AM receiving abundance now in expected and unexpected ways.

I AM increasingly confident in my ability to create the life I desire.

I AM acting on inspiration and insights and I trust my inner guidance.

I AM giving and receiving all that is good and all that I desire.

I AM receiving infinite, inexhaustible and immediate abundance.

I AM creating my life according to my dominant beliefs; and I AM improving the quality of those beliefs.

I AM constantly striving to raise my vibration through good thoughts, words and actions.

I AM making a meaningful contribution to the world and I AM wonderfully compensated for my contribution.

I AM willing to believe that I AM the creator of my life experience.

I AM willing to believe that by raising my vibration, I will attract more of what I desire.

I AM willing to believe that by focusing on feeling good, I make better choices that lead to desired results.

Money comes to me easily and effortlessly.

I constantly attract opportunities that create more money.

I am worthy of making more money.

I am open and receptive to all the wealth life offers me.

My actions create constant prosperity.

Money and spirituality can co-exist in harmony.

I am full of positive loving energy.

I welcome love and romance into my life.

I am in a loving and supportive relationship.

I deserve love and I get it in abundance.

I am loved, loving and lovable.

I am blessed with an incredible family and wonderful friends.

I give out love and it is returned to me multiplied many fold.

I forgive myself and set myself free.

I believe I can be all that I want to be.

I am in the process of becoming the best version of myself.

I have the freedom & power to create the life I desire.

I choose to be kind to myself and love myself unconditionally.

My possibilities are endless.

I am worthy of my dreams.

I am enough.

I deserve to be healthy and feel good.

I am full of energy and vitality and my mind is calm and peaceful.

Every day I am getting healthier and stronger.

I honour my body by trusting the signals that it sends me.

I manifest perfect health by making smart choices.

I am grateful to be alive. It is my joy and pleasure to live another wonderful day.

Happiness is my birth right. I choose to be happy and I deserve to be happy.

Being happy comes easy to me. Happiness is my second nature.

Good things are happening.

I am deeply fulfilled by what I do.

I have unlimited power at my disposal."

"I have an unlimited mindset."

"I am more powerful than I appear to be."

"I am joy."

I know my wisdom and experiences guide me to the right decision.

I look my options objectively and then make the best decision for me.

I make the right decision always.

I receive all advice and feedback with grateful kindness, but I make the final decision myself.

I trust myself to make the best decisions.

I am love."

"I am kindness."

"I am strong."

"I am powerful."

"I am infinite."

"I am super human."

"I am superman."

"I am a titan."

"I am ruthless in execution."

"I am radiating success."

I am a winner who is destined for greatness."

"I am discovering my greatness day by day."

"I have awakened to my greatness."

"I am the best at what I do."

"I am a game changer."

"I am blessed."

"I am all that I am."

"I am me."

"I am destined to accomplish great things in my life."

I am a light that gives hope, inspiration, and belief to others to achieve their dreams.

I create my life on a quantum level. There are endless opportunities.

I have a healthy body, tranquil mind and a vibrant soul.

I am enough.

I don't entertain negativity in any shape or form. I simply let it go.

I love the fact that so many people have faith in me.

I create happiness by appreciating the little things in life.

I am blessed to have a wonderful family and friends.

I embrace the rhythm of life and let it unfold.

I focus on action to create the life I want. The smallest step can end years of stagnation.

I know my intuition will always take me in the right direction.

I adore my quirks because they make me unique.

I can become anything I put my mind to.

I believe in my dreams and I won't stop until they become real

I have nothing to fear because I can seek guidance whenever I want.

I always give when I can because I know it always comes back.

I see failure as a golden opportunity to learn.

I know that massive action cures everything.

I love the creative energy that flows through me.

I work for my desires because I don't want regret.

I don't live for things, I live for a spiritual purpose.

emanate love and joy, complete presence and openness, toward all beings.

I focus not on the 100 things I may have to do at some future time, but on the one thing I can do NOW.

I do not pollute my beautiful, radiant Inner Being, nor the Earth, with negativity. I do not give unhappiness, in any form, whatsoever, a dwelling place inside me.

I perceive another person's body and mind as just a screen, behind which I can feel their true reality, just as I feel mine.

I am content with what I have. I rejoice in the way things are. I realize that there is nothing lacking. The whole world belongs to me.

My peace is so vast and so deep, that anything that is NOT peace, disappears into it, as if it had never existed.

Nothing that was ever done to me, or which I did to others, can touch, even in the slightest, the radiant essence of who I really am.

I am powerful enough to overcome negativity.

I am creative enough to express myself.

All problems are illusions of the mind.

I have the ability to accomplish any task I set my mind to with ease and comfort.

I have infinite patience when it comes to fulfilling my destiny.

I am a Divine creation, a piece of God. Therefore, I cannot be undeserving.

I am connected to an unlimited source of abundance.

I have access to unlimited assistance. My strength comes from my connection to my Source of being.

I am an infinite being. The age of my body has no bearing on what I do or who I am.

I live in the present moment by being grateful for all of my life experiences as a child.

As I unclutter my life, I free myself to answer the callings of my soul.

Being myself involves no risks. It's my ultimate truth, and I live fearlessly.

I live in the moment and am grateful for all my life experiences. All of them.

relax and cast aside all mental burdens, allowing God to express through me His perfect love, peace, and wisdom.

The healing power of Spirit is flowing through all the cells of my body. I am made of the one universal God-substance.

God's perfect health permeates the dark nooks of my bodily sickness. In all my cells His healing light is shining. They are entirely well, for His perfection is in them.

Daily I will seek happiness more and more within my mind, and less and less through material pleasures.

God is the shepherd of my restless thoughts. He will lead them to His abode of peace.

I will purify my mind with the thought that God is guiding my every activity.

With the sword of devotion, I sever the heart-strings that tie me to delusion. With the deepest love, I lay my heart at the feet of Omnipresence.

I am submerged in eternal light. It permeates every particle of my being. I am living in that light. The Divine Spirit fills me within and without.

God is within and around me, protecting me; so I will banish the fear that shuts out His guiding light.

I will help weeping ones to smile, by smiling myself, even when it is difficult.

My mind and body are in complete alignment with the Universe and I am always in the flow.

I am responsible for my own spiritual growth.

I trust that everything in my life is working for my highest good and I am receiving all that I am meant to have.

When I love people more, I receive even more love from them in return.

I am a divine expression of a loving God.

I let go of fear. I let go of pain. I live in love.

I am a loving, kind and forgiving person, in accordance with my spiritual nature.

I ask for forgiveness from all those whom I may have wronged and forgive all those who may have wronged me. All is well.

The love of God flows through me. I am His, He is mine.

I surrender to God. He is always with me. I do only his bidding.

Religion to me is a way of life. It is a way of living a morally and ethically correct life

Positive healing energy flows easily through me.

I am open to receiving divine healing.

I surrender pain and suffering.

I take good care of myself.

I feel divine healing.

My body is a holy temple.

I am well taken care of by God.

I receive the healing presence of God.

Life loves me!

All is well in my world. Everything is working out for my highest good. Out of this situation only good will come. I am safe!

It's only a thought, and a thought can be changed.

The point of power is always in the present moment.

Every thought we think is creating our future.

I am in the process of positive change.

I am comfortable looking in the mirror, saying, "I love you, I really love you."

It is safe to look within.

I forgive myself and set myself free.

As I say yes to life, life says yes to me.

I now go beyond other people's fears and limitations.

I am Divinely guided and protected at all times.

I claim my power and move beyond all limitations.

I trust the process of life.

I am deeply fulfilled by all that I do.

We are all family, and the planet is our home.

As I forgive myself, it becomes easier to forgive others.

I am willing to let go.

Deep at the center of my being is an infinite well of love.

I prosper wherever I turn.

I welcome miracles into my life.

Whatever I need to know is revealed to me at exactly the right time.

I am loved, and I am at peace.

My happy thoughts help create my healthy body.

Life supports me in every possible way.

My day begins and ends with gratitude.

I listen with love to my body's messages.

The past is over.

Only good can come to me.

I am beautiful, and everybody loves me.

Everyone I encounter today has my best interests at heart.

I always work with and for wonderful people. I love my job.

Filling my mind with pleasant thoughts is the quickest road to health.

I am healthy, whole, and complete.

I am at home in my body.

I devote a portion of my time to helping others. It is good for my own health.

I am greeted by love wherever I go.

Wellness is the natural state of my body. I am in perfect health.

I am pain free and totally in sync with life.

I am very thankful for all the love in my life. I find it everywhere.

I know that old, negative patterns no longer limit me. I let them go with ease.

In the infinity of life where I am, all is perfect, whole, and complete.

I trust my intuition. I am willing to listen to that still, small voice within.

I am willing to ask for help when I need it.

I forgive myself for not being perfect.

I honor who I am.

I attract only healthy relationships. I am always treated well.

I do not have to prove myself to anyone.

I come from the loving space of my heart, and I know that love opens all doors.

I am in harmony with nature.

I welcome new ideas.

Today, no person, place, or thing can irritate or annoy me. I choose to be at peace.

I am safe in the Universe and All Life loves and supports me.

I experience love wherever I go.

I am willing to change.

I drink lots of water to cleanse my body and mind.

I choose to see clearly with the eyes of love.

I cross all bridges with joy and ease.

I release all drama from my life.

Loving others is easy when I love and accept myself.

I balance my life between work, rest, and play.

I return to the basics of life: forgiveness, courage, gratitude, love, and humor.

I am in charge, I now take my own power back.

My body appreciates how I take care of it.

I spend time with positive, energetic people.

The more peaceful I am inside, the more peace I have to share with others.

Today is a sacred gift from Life.

I have the courage to live my dreams.

I release all negative thoughts of the past and all worries about the future.

I forgive everyone in my past for all perceived wrongs. I release them with love.

I only speak positively about those in my world. Negativity has no part in my life.

We are all eternal spirit.

I act as if I already have what I want—it's an excellent way to attract happiness in my life.

I enjoy the foods that are best for my body.

My life gets better all the time.

It is safe for me to speak up for myself.

I live in the paradise of my own creation.

Perfect health is my Divine right, and I claim it now.

I release all criticism.

I am on an ever-changing journey.

I am grateful for my healthy body. I love life.

Love flows through my body, healing all dis-ease.

My income is constantly increasing.

My healing is already in process.

There is always more to learn.

I now live in limitless love, light, and joy.

I become more lovable every day.

It is now safe for me to release all of my childhood traumas and move into love.

I deserve all that is good.

I am constantly discovering new ways to improve my health.

Love is all there is!

My life gets more fabulous every day.

Today I am at peace.

Loving others is easy when I love and accept myself.

I have the perfect living space.

I have compassion for all.

I trust the Universe to help me see the good in everything and in everyone.

I love my family members just as they are. I do not try to change anyone.

There is plenty for everyone, and we bless and prosper each other.

I love and approve of myself.

Life is good, and so it is!

I always attract the best and most interesting people.

I am a good friend.

I am a unique person that has a lot to offer a friendship.

I am confident and friendly.

I ask others to spend time with me.

I reach out to others realizing I can meet their needs.

I will be myself in my relationships and relax, knowing I am likable.

I will respond to those who come into my life today with understanding and joy.

It is alright to feel lonely sometimes.

I feel motivated and am moving in the direction of my dreams.
I have unlimited creativity, drive and motivation.
I am motivated to continue perusing my goals.

New opportunities are showing up daily and I am inspired to take action towards those opportunities.

I feel alive, energized and motivated to take on any task in front of me.

I am continually re-energized and share that enthusiasm with others.

Motivation comes easily to me.

Staying motivated comes easily to me.

Because of my profound energy, I achieve and exceed at all that I do.

I am so motivated that others get inspired just by being around me.

I attract those that help me reach my goals.

I am motivated and live my life to the fullest.

My life is full of purpose and motivation.

I have unlimited energy and motivation.

I am happy and motivated when I achieve my goals.

I am easily motivated.

I easily stay motivated toward my dreams.

I stay motivated and energized when working toward my goals.

I wake up energized and ready to face the day.

I am confident in what I do and that keeps me motivated to continue moving forward.

> I am perfectly healthy, my body is in great shape, and I am beaming with energy.

> I am enjoying an abundance of energy and I am feeling so healthy both physically and mentally.

> I release myself from all negative energy and align myself with pure, fun, and positive energy.

> Every day in every way, I am getting healthier and healthier, and feeling better and better.

I love myself and I am perfectly healthy in every way possible.

I always feel good and as a result, my body feels good and I radiate good feelings.

Good health is my birth right. I bless my body every single day and take good care of it.

I have a strong heart and a steel body. I am vigorous, energetic, and full of vitality.

I treat my body as a temple. It is holy, it is clean and it is full of goodness.

I breathe deeply, exercise regularly and feed only good nutritious food to my body.

To start your day with a strong and healthy relationship:

I am in a loving relationship filled with unconditional love, trust, and respect.

I have a wonderful partner, and we are both happy and at peace.

I am in a joyous intimate relationship with a person who truly loves me.

I enjoy the time I spend with my spouse and we have fun together.

I love that my marriage is becoming deeper, stronger, and more loving every day.

I love that my relationship is becoming more romantic every day.

I enjoy being loved and treasured by my amazing, kind, and generous partner.

I am the best friend anyone can have because I am loyal, loving, and understanding.

I choose friends who love me the way I am and approve of me.

I show my family how much I love them in every way possible – both verbal and non-verbal.

I forgive everyone in my past for all perceived wrongs. I release them with love.

To start your day with abundance and success:

I am a money magnet. Money flows to me easily and effortlessly.

I am open and receptive to all the wealth life offers me.

I use money to better my life and the lives of others.

I constantly attract opportunities that create more money.

My finances improve beyond my wildest dreams.

Every day in every way, I receive more and more money.

Whatever activities I perform make money for me and I am always full of money.

Every day I am attracting and saving more and more money.

I attract money naturally. My middle name is money.

I am deserving of abundance in my life.

I am open to receive wealth in many ways.

The more I give, the more I receive. The more I receive, the more I give.

My life is full of love and joy and all the material things that I need.

Prosperity overflows in my life. I have everything in abundance.

I allow all good things to come into my life and I enjoy them.

Right now, I accept the abundance that is flowing into my life.

I celebrate the abundance of others knowing that my joy in celebration increases my own abundance.

To start your day with hope, confidence, and feeling positive:

Every day is a new day full of hopes, happiness, and possibilities.

As I say yes to life, life says yes to me.

I claim my power and move beyond all limitations.

I am beautiful, and everybody loves me.

I am very thankful for all the love in my life. I find it everywhere.

I am greeted by love wherever I go.

I am safe in the Universe and All Life loves and supports me.

My thoughts are my reality so I think up a bright new day.

There is plenty for everyone, and we bless and prosper each other.

When my intentions are clear, the Universe cooperates with me and I can accomplish anything.

I think of only positive things and positive things happen in my life.

I am full of energy and hope and live my life to the fullest.

Motivation comes to me from inside. I am my own motivator.

I know that I have the knowledge and resources to achieve my dreams.

I fully accept myself and know that I am worthy of great things in life.

I am destined for big success in life.

I am recognized as an expert in my industry for my pioneering work.

To start your day free of worry, stress, and negative feelings:

I easily release all tension from my mind and body.

I am beginning to live a more balanced and peaceful life.

Every day I become more peaceful and content.

My mind is becoming calm and clear.

I am working calmly towards resolving my worries and concerns.

I easily meet and overcome challenges.

I release my fear of failure. I am motivated by love, always.

To start your day with greatness and motivation:

I feel motivated and am moving in the direction of my dreams.

I am motivated to continue perusing my goals.

I feel alive, energized and motivated to take on any task in front of me.

I am continually re-energized and share that enthusiasm with others.

Because of my profound energy, I achieve and exceed at all that I do.

I am so motivated that others get inspired just by being around me.

I am confident in what I do and that keeps me motivated to continue moving forward.

I am motivated and live my life to the fullest.

To start your day focusing on your work and career:

Right now, I am working at my dream job.

I am a valued person at my workplace and my voice is always heard respectfully.

I have a great relationship with my colleagues as well as my boss.

I am a born entrepreneur. I recognize and seize opportunities as and when they appear.

I engage in work that impacts this world positively.

I am creating the career of my dreams. It appears in my mind and then in my world.

As I align my career with my true talents, the money and the happiness flows to me!

CONCLUSION

Lastly, if you enjoyed this audiobook I ask that you please take the time to review it on Audible.com. Your honest feedback would be greatly appreciated.

Thank you.

Now, I would like to share with you a free sneak peek to another one of my audiobooks that I think you will really enjoy. The audiobook is called "Rapid Weight Loss, Fat Burn and Calorie Blast with Powerful Affirmations" Published by PMT Publishing.

It's an audiobook that provides you with affirmations to Condition Your Mind and Body to Naturally Lose Weight. I will help you to Look Amazing, Stay Fit and Healthy for Life.

Enjoy!

Stay Fit Affirmations

- Breathing in, I feel healthy. Breathing out, I AM healthy.
- Step by step and rep by rep, I am creating my ideal body!
- Today I choose health and wellness over illness in my life.
- I am fit! I am healthy! I am strong!
- When I eat right, I feel right!
- The more water I drink the better I feel!
- My life is what I make of it and today I choose to make it healthy place to be.
- No sugar for me! My immune system is healthy, strong, and protecting me right now!
- When I feel good, I exercise. When I exercise, I feel good.
- Today and every day, I cleanse my being with the life force of my breath.
- I AM healthy in mind, body, and spirit!
- My body is a marvelous machine that supports and meets my every need!
- Day by day, my body is transforming into the vision I have for it.
- Today I am healthy, strong, and disease-free!
- I am strong, vibrant, and healthy!
- Today and every day, I express my gratitude for my good health.
- Today I am blessed by the beautiful and delicious food that brings me to full health!
- My pain is limited to my body. I am constantly connected to something far greater than my body.
- As my reasons for holding on to my excess weight melt away, so does the weight.

- Today I am shedding the pounds as I shred my self doubt.
- Today nothing, and I mean nothing, stands between me and my goal weight. I am there before I know it!
- Day by day, I am losing the weight and the people around me are taking notice.
- My heart beats strong and healthy!
- My lungs breathe clear and strong!
- Day in and day out, I develop the habits of health!
- My body is the very picture of health and vitality!
- Today I am shedding pounds as i shred my self-doubt!
- My body is a well-oiled machine ready to meet my every need!
- I pay attention to the needs of my body. I feed it, exercise it, and love it!
- Today I push my limits in the gym so that tomorrow I can push the limits in my life!
- Today my own well-being is my top priority.
- Today I love my body fully, deeply and joyfully.

- My body has its own wisdom and I trust that wisdom completely.

- My body is simply a projection of my beliefs about myself.

- I am growing more beautiful and luminous day by day.

- I choose to see the divine perfection in every cell of my body.

- As I love myself, I allow others to love me too.

- Flaws are transformed by love and acceptance.

- Today I choose to honor my beauty, my strength and my uniqueness.
- I love the way I feel when I take good care of myself.
- Today I am transforming my body into calorie-burning machine.
- As my self-confidence rises, the number on the scale drops!
- Who I am transcends a number on a scale! Today I focus on my health not my weight!
- Today I experience vibrant health and profound well-being!
- Even at the height of my pain, I experience moments of release, contentment, and joy.
- I may have to live with pain, but I absolutely refuse to be defined by it!
- I love and accept myself at my current weight, even as I march pound by pound to my goal weight!
- My contributions to life measure my self-worth not the scale!
- Happiness is an attitude not a number on a scale! I refuse to be defined by my weight!
- I beyond the need for food to fill me up. My life is full of people and activities that do it.
- I cannot lose 100 pounds this week, but I CAN lose three pounds and I AM!
- Today I see myself at my goal weight. I feel my feelings at my goal weight. I see the clothes I wear. I see the experiences I have. I hear the compliments I receive. Today I am my goal weight. Today I am my goal weight. Today I am my goal weight.
- Day by day, I am transforming my body into a high performance machine!

- My weight loss is within me. My diet is only a tool to get me to my goal.
- As I commit to my exercise program, I transform my body!
- Step by step and rep by rep, I am losing pounds and inches today!
- A fit, healthy person lives within me. Today that person emerges.
- Today I eat for my goal weight! Today I exercise for my goal weight! Today I AM my goal weight!
- The more I bike the better I feel and the better I feel the more I bike!
- The more I run, the better I feel and the better I feel the more I run!
- I am slender, strong, and perfectly conditioned.
- The longer I exercise the stronger I get and the stronger I get the longer I exercise!
- I am an immaculate being of light. Perfect in form and function. My body is a marvelous machine that supports and meets my every need.
- My weight is meaningless in the big picture. Today I release the need to weigh one pound more than I want to!
- Pound by pound, inch by inch, choice by choice I am becoming healthy and fit!
- I struggle, but I grow. I fall, but I get up. Even amid adversity, I keep moving towards my goal weight.
- Today my portion size is shrinking and so is my waistline.
- I am beautiful, I am fit, I am healthy; and more so every day!
- Today I am making the choices and the changes to have the body I want!

- Today and every day, I feel the momentum building in my life for a healthy, fit lifestyle.
- I love my body and today I treat it with the respect it deserves.
- I deserve a healthy, fit body and today I claim it!
- Today I weigh less than yesterday and tomorrow I weigh even less!
- Today I am seeing the new, slimmer me in the mirror and I love that!
- Today I am making peace with food. Food nourishes my body, but I nourish my soul!
- All excess fat is melting away from my body.
- All my work-outs are concentrated and intense.
- As my body becomes slimmer I feel a great sense of lightness and freedom.
- Being fit and vital is one of the top priorities in my life.
- Daily exercise makes me feel fantastic!
- Daily exercise makes me healthy and attractive.
- Dancing improves my vitality and frees my soul.
- Every action I take moves me towards my perfect body.
- Every day I become more agile and lithe.
- Every day I get maximum results by increasing the intensity of my work outs.
- Every day I look slimmer and firmer.
- Every day I maximize my physical potential.
- Every day my body becomes slimmer and firmer.
- Every day my body becomes stronger and leaner.
- Every day my body becomes younger and fitter.
- Every day my muscles become stronger and more defined.
- Every day my muscles grow stronger and firmer.

- Every moment of every day I am becoming leaner and fitter.
- Every physical activity I take part in, helps me to reach my ideal weight.
- Every time I exercise I build more muscle and burn more fat.
- Exercise does as much for my mental state as it does for my body.
- Exercise greatly improves my positive self image.
- Exercise is the best stress reliever ever invented.
- Exercise makes my body feel powerful and vital.
- Exercise releases endorphins, which makes me a happier person.
- Exercise revitalizes my body and refreshes my mind.
- Exercise tones up my body and tunes up my self-esteem.
- Exercising daily gives me incredible energy.
- Exercising daily improves my mood.
- Exercising is fun and revitalizing.
- Exercising is one of my favorite stress relievers.
- Exercising is rejuvenating; it brings me abundant energy.
- I always find the time to exercise.
- I always look for opportunities to exercise my body.
- I always make the time to improve my body.

Thank you for listening, this preview is now over.

I hope you enjoyed this preview of my audiobook "Rapid Weight Loss, Fat Burn and Calorie Blast with Powerful Affirmations" Published by PMT Publishing.

Please make sure to check out the full audiobook on Audible.com

Thank you for listening.

www.ingramcontent.com/pod-product-compliance
Lightning Source LLC
Chambersburg PA
CBHW030108100526
44591CB00009B/326